50 Years of Technical Education in Singapore

How to Build a World Class TVET System

World Scientific Series on Singapore's 50 Years of Nation-Building

---

The complete list of titles in the series can be found at
http://www.worldscientific.com/series/wss50ynb

World Scientific Series on
Singapore's 50 Years of Nation-Building

50 YEARS OF TECHNICAL EDUCATION IN SINGAPORE

How to Build a World Class TVET System

N. Varaprasad

Singapore Education Consulting Group

World Scientific

NEW JERSEY · LONDON · SINGAPORE · BEIJING · SHANGHAI · HONG KONG · TAIPEI · CHENNAI · TOKYO

Published by

World Scientific Publishing Co. Pte. Ltd.

5 Toh Tuck Link, Singapore 596224

USA office: 27 Warren Street, Suite 401-402, Hackensack, NJ 07601

UK office: 57 Shelton Street, Covent Garden, London WC2H 9HE

Library of Congress Cataloging-in-Publication Data
Varaprasad, N. (Natarajan)
    50 years of technical education in Singapore : how to build a world class TVET system /
N Varaprasad.
        pages cm. -- (World scientific series on Singapore's 50 years of nation-building)
    Includes bibliographical references and index.
    ISBN 978-9814699594 (hardcover : alk. paper) -- ISBN 978-9814704335 (pbk.)
    1. Vocational education--Singapore--History. 2. Technical education--Singapore--History.
I. Title.
    LC1047.S55V37 2015
    373.246095957--dc23
                                                                            2015029799

British Library Cataloguing-in-Publication Data
A catalogue record for this book is available from the British Library.

Typeset by Stallion Press
Email: enquiries@stallionpress.com

This book is dedicated to all those fearless but under-appreciated pioneers who took technical education in Singapore from nothing to its status as a global gold standard today and to those visionaries who could see the future when it was both dark and distant.

I would like to dedicate this book to the memory of the late Dr Tay Eng Soon, Senior Minister of State for Education, who was Minister in charge of VITB, ITE and the Polytechnics for his untiring efforts to raise the profile of TVET in Singapore and thereby secure good jobs for hundreds of thousands of humble Singaporeans.

Contents

Foreword

Mr Heng Swee Keat
Former Minister for Education (2011–2015)

Our technical and vocational education system is a point of pride for our Singapore education system. Education experts and specialists come from around the world to visit the three colleges of the Institute of Technical Education (ITE) and our five polytechnics. They admire the facilities, and the wide range of quality, relevant courses offered.

Our technical and vocational education system is also a personal point of pride for me. I have hosted Heads of State and Prime Ministers in these institutions, and, every time, they have come away impressed, not just by the facilities or the courses, but by the spirit and abilities of our students. Our polytechnics and ITE are the post-secondary landscape where around 70% of each cohort discover their strengths and learn the skills that enable them to pursue active, productive and meaningful careers and lives.

One of my favourite "duties" while I was at the Ministry of Education was to join in the graduation ceremonies of ITE and our polytechnics — there is no mistaking the pride of the students and their families at their achievements, or the sense of promise and confidence with which they step out with what they have learnt to make a difference in the world. It is always a cause of great joy for all of us when the students excel.

It took us several decades of experimentation and learning to develop the vibrant technical and vocational education system we see today. We are fortunate today to be able to build on the foundations laid by early pioneers in this field. Each year, I see our institutions continually improving, working ever harder to draw a closer nexus between the diverse aspirations of young Singaporeans and the ever evolving opportunities in our economy.

This book helps to document the story of technical education in Singapore. It is a story of how we have created opportunities for our people, young and old. It is a story that prompts us to reflect on where we have done well, and where we can improve. I hope this may also be of some value for other countries going through the same journey.

Dr N Varaprasad, has spent sixteen years in the polytechnic sector in Singapore, including eleven as the founding Principal of Temasek Polytechnic. His account covers Singapore's colonial legacy and the steps we took to enable our people to catch the wave of rapid industrialisation in the 1960s and early 70s. The book offers some policy lessons for others who are going through the same cycle of development, or are planning to do so. It also introduces SkillsFuture, which aims to prepare Singapore's workforce for rapid and profound economic changes to come.

I would like to take this opportunity to salute our pioneers in this field, from the days of TED, AEB, ITB and VITB, to our ITE and the Polytechnics today. They have all made a very significant contribution to the success of our education system and to our young people.

Preface

Technical and Vocational Education and Training (better known as TVET in many parts of the world) is recognised as one of Singapore's success stories from an overseas perspective, and as a critical contributory factor (amongst others) to the economic and social development of this island nation.

This focus on education as a strategic tool of national development, bringing with it valued and positive changes in the social and economic status of the population, is a post-World War II phenomenon. After World War II, the Japanese industrial renaissance demonstrated that education and skills were essential for rapid and planned economic growth. The development of human resources to its fullest is now widely accepted as a strategic tool for socio-economic development, particularly in promoting industrialisation and technological upgrading. This utilitarian view is particularly strong in developing countries today which had placed less emphasis on skills and more on tertiary education at the university level.

It is easy to attribute the success of the Singapore TVET story to a strong education ethic in the population and unstinting government support in developing this sector to its fullest in a small country without natural resources. So it will come as some surprise to many that the road has not actually been a smooth one. In getting to the present scenario of a well-accepted and highly respected TVET sector, there have been many twists and turns and debates among policy makers to bridge the gap between immediate needs and long-term requirements. Only in the present state of perceived stability does it all appear to have come together as a coherent strategy. Even now, nothing is static and progress have towards the future will mean further changes of direction.

This book is a record of the history of the rise and rise of technical and vocational education in Singapore. Even though it is written to commemorate Singapore's 50th anniversary of independence, it does not limit itself to the last fifty years.

TVET in Singapore has closely paralleled the economic growth phases of the nation. From 1959 until the mid-1970s, the economic strategy was to gain a foothold at the lowest rung of the production chain of industry and manufacturing to create mass employment. This saw a period of expansion of schooling as well as fast-tracked basic technical education to feed the demands of a fast-growing manufacturing base.

With unemployment no longer an issue, from the mid-1970s to the 1990s, there was a rapid shift to a capital-intensive high technology strategy, requiring higher level of skills. MNCs were urged and incentivised to establish training institutes, not just for themselves but also for the rest of the industry. This created quality models of technical education that imparted high technology in precision engineering, robotics, software engineering and so on. Nevertheless, the numbers that were entering polytechnics and universities were still below what was needed. Hence new polytechnics were established, and the VITB was upgraded to the ITE.

The third phase of economic development commenced in the mid-1990s when the shift to R&D, innovation, creativity and services took place. This would take Singapore to the top end of the value chain, developing new technologies, new biomedical and biologic products and high value services. Technical education was repositioned to become a fully post-secondary option, and facilities and curricula were upgraded. Creativity, innovation and problem-solving were better integrated into the curriculum.

As this book is being written, technical education is moving towards developing deeper skills, apprenticeship schemes are making a comeback, and the emphasis is towards mastery, rather than swift career changes. The line between degree-holders and non-degree-holders is being blurred and a better balance between academic achievements and deep skills is the long-range goal.

This book will be of interest to government officials and educationists all over the world who are concerned with formulating policy with an eye to economic development. The returns from TVET to economic and social development are significant especially in developing economies. Hence this book begins in Chapter 1 with an account of the attitudes and conditions against developing industrial skills that prevailed during the colonial period and how these were regularly reinforced by the colonial government. These attitudes towards developing skills and trades had to be radically exorcised post-independence and new progressive thinking aligned to the priorities of the newly-independent state was urgently imposed.

In Chapter 2, we see how the new government, on assuming power on an electoral platform of raising living standards and reducing unemployment, had to establish its education priorities on a limited budget. The task of nation-building and economic development provided an opportunity for the government to introduce some notion of hands-on skills into the mainstream curriculum notably for girls as well as boys.

Chapter 3 documents the various policy actions that were introduced to promote technical and vocational education. A number of study teams and committees were variously formed and produced a plethora of reports. This was a period of trial and error and quick change as the new government was on a steep learning curve, trying to adapt the inherited systems. The mainstream TVET system began to take shape. Several vocational institutes were opened in many parts of the nation-state and became part of the school system. However, these institutes did not attract good students and were aimed at keeping the weaker students in the education system.

One of the interesting and more innovative developments is documented in Chapter 4, namely getting the foreign MNCs that were investing in Singapore to themselves invest in the training to create the workforce they needed. This was a brilliant move which ensured that competent technical staff was continually being readied for the companies as well as for the larger economy.

Chapter 5 is devoted to the development of the polytechnic sector, which started in pre-independence 1954. However, it was not until the 1970s that the mission of the polytechnics was formalized and they began to expand on their own steam. By the end of the millennium, there were five full-fledged polytechnics with an enrolment exceeding 50,000 students and competing robustly with the more academic junior colleges for good students.

Notwithstanding the success of vocational education, the real transformation took place in the early 2000s, when vocational education became a post-secondary institution with the repositioning of the Vocational and Industrial Training Board as the Institute of Technical Education and the building of three mega campuses to rival the polytechnics. This gave technical and vocational education pride of place in the educational landscape. Together with other innovations, vocational education in Singapore was finally transformed. This transformation story is narrated in Chapter 6.

The working population, many of whom did not reap the benefits of universal education, was also called upon to become technically more proficient and to upgrade its skills. How this massive task of training 1.7 million workers was achieved is described in Chapter 7. The labour movement moved mountains, employers and the government to achieve this Herculean task, and credit goes to the system of tripartism and visionary leadership.

The Singapore education system provides multiple pathways to higher educa-tion, and this is one of the reasons why the technical pathway is well-accepted by parents and students. This system of bridges and ladders is described in Chapter 8, these have in recent times have been widened and strengthened to provide more opportunities for upgrading and career advancement.

In Chapter 9, the cycle comes full circle with the ASPIRE report of 2014, re-emphasising the role of mastery of skills in the economic ecosystem. Looking ahead at the new normal in developed economies, post the 2007 global financial crisis, with high graduate unemployment and the ensuing social unrest, the govern-ment has sent a strong signal about the value of skills and competencies, rather than mere paper qualifications.

Finally the book concludes with some policy lessons that are drawn from the Singapore experience in building TVET. While many countries continue to model Germany and Switzerland for their vaunted apprenticeship-based skill prepara-tion, the Singapore model is increasingly the subject of study and emulation. Hence this summary would benefit policy-makers who do not wish to read the historical narrative in detail.

The story of technical education in Singapore is not linear but one marked by constant re-evaluation and bold changes. Fifty years may be a short time in the history of a nation but for the players involved, it has been an exciting and fulfilling journey to ensure that the young are always better trained and prepared for the future than the preceding generation.

In preparing this book, there are many people to thank. First and foremost are the pioneer leaders of the TVET system who consented to be interviewed, among them Mr Lim Jit Poh, the first Director of VITB, Mr Khoo Kay Chai, first Singaporean Principal of Singapore Polytechnic, Mr Chen Hung, Principal of Ngee Ann Polytechnic during its major expansion in the 1980s, Mr Lee Keh Sai who has contributed immensely to the development of TVET in Singapore in many capaci-ties, Mr Bob Tan and Mr Bruce Poh, Chairman and Director of ITE respectively. I have also to thank Dr Law Song Seng, former Director of VITB and the first Director of ITE who had documented the transformation of TVET in Singapore during his tenure.

I would be remiss if I did not acknowledge the assistance of the staff of the Lee Kong Chian Reference Library of the National Library, in particular Ms Chow Wun Han and her team. Next, I thank Ms V Prema and Ms Evelyn Chong for supporting the writing and proofreading and making valuable suggestions. The final product is also the outcome of the editorial team at World Scientific who worked tirelessly to bring out a quality series for this golden jubilee of Singapore.

And most importantly, my dear wife Chitra for her patience and understanding in having a half-absent husband for the duration of the writing, and going on holidays on her own, which was a new but uplifting and enlightening experience for her.

Dr N. Varaprasad
January 2016

CHAPTER 1

The Colonial Legacy

Landmark Events:

1902: Report of the Commission of Enquiry into the System of English Education in the Colony (the Kynnerseley Report)

1919: Report of the Committee on Technical and Industrial Education in the Federated Malay States (the Lemon Report)

1925: Report of the Technical Education Committee (the Winstedt Report)

1929: First Government Trade School opens in Scotts Road

1938: Report on Vocational Education in Malaya (the Cheeseman Report)

1938: St Joseph's Trade School opened

1948: Government Trade School moves to Balestier

1951: Report of the Committee on a Polytechnic Institute for Singapore (the Dobby Report)

1951: Government Trade School becomes Balestier Junior Technical School

1954: Establishment of Singapore Polytechnic

1956: Joint Advisory Council for Apprenticeship Training

1956: Tanjong Katong and Queenstown Technical Secondary Schools established

1959: Official Opening of Singapore Polytechnic

1959: Internal self-government status for Singapore

1959: Dr Toh Chin Chye becomes Chairman of Singapore Polytechnic; emphasis on training for jobs and closure of academic, commercial and evening courses.

1963: Merger with Malaysia

1965: Independence

Although the main theme and attention of this book is the development of Technical Education in Singapore from independence in 1965 onwards, it is instructive to rewind to the state of play before that. Many developing and emerging economies and nations would be able to identify with this period when colonial attitudes and prejudices created legacy systems and mindsets that became ingrained and difficult to change later, especially regarding education that served the colonial service and not the state's growing needs nor the individual's economic mobility.

Singapore was under British colonial rule from 1819 to 1955, when partial self-government status (1955–1959) followed by full self-government (1959–1963) including power over education policy was given to the elected local government. Between 1963 to 1965, there was a short-lived period when Singapore was part of the larger political entity of Malaysia, and full independence and sovereignty began only from August 9, 1965.

Therefore independent Singapore had authority over educational matters from 1955 onwards. However, the period that followed was one of political turmoil and infighting and there was little attention paid to educational matters. It was only in 1959, when the People's Action Party (PAP) won with a strong mandate to govern, that changes began to be put in place.

Therefore the half-century before 1965 could be divided into roughly three phases:

(a) Until 1948 — the deep colonial period, pre-and post World War II;
(b) Between 1948 and 1959 — the period of local awakening; and
(c) Between 1959 and 1965 — the self-governing period and merger.

The Deep Colonial Period

It was not that technical education was not on the agenda of the colonial government. Indeed, there were many committees, studies and reports on the subject. The 1902 Kynnerseley Report of the Commission of Enquiry into the System of English Education in the Colony, for example, stated that suggestions had been received by the Commission for a technical and commercial school in Singapore, separate from the existing schools, which would teach engineering, surveying, medicine, and assaying amongst other subjects. However, it concluded that there did not appear to be sufficient demand to warrant a separate school. In 1917, Winstedt, after a survey of schools in the Dutch East Indies and the Philippines, recommended that a trade school be established first in Kuala Lumpur, but not in Singapore.

In September of the same year, the Straits Chinese British Association passed a resolution "that in their opinion, the time has now arrived when the Government should promote higher education by endowing scholarships or preferably, by starting a technical school". The Chinese representative in the Legislative Council,

Dr Lim Boon Keng, handed the resolution to the government. Hence in 1918, the government appointed A.H. Lemon to head a committee on this matter, covering the whole of the Federated Malay States, including Singapore.

The Lemon Committee report of 1919 reviewed the need for technical and industrial education and made solid recommendations for the establishment of more English elementary schools; the establishment of trade schools using Malay as a medium of instruction; the building of a new technical school with English as the medium of instruction; the provision of an agricultural school; raising the salaries of technical staff to match their clerical counterparts in the colonial service; and the establishment of an English teachers' training college.

None of these far-sighted and far-reaching recommendations ever saw the light of day. In the Annual Report of 1924 of the Department of Education, the Director for Education admitted that the subject of technical and industrial education was the most difficult and debatable subject in his department. So it is no surprise that another esteemed committee was formed by the Governor of the Straits Settlements to study the issue and make its recommendations.

In 1925, the Report of the Technical Education Committee (the Winstedt Report) was submitted. This report makes for very interesting reading as it reveals not only the colonial mentality towards the local population, but also how the purpose of education is viewed. It also provides a glimpse into the ethnic stereotyping and profiling that passed for good judgment.

For example, paragraph 7 of this report reads as follows:

> 7. *We are not sanguine that a technical branch at Raffles College will be successful,*
>
> (i) *until the struggle for existence grows more acute and the openings in agriculture and commerce for an increasing population fewer;*
>
> (ii) *until applied mathematics, drawing, manual instruction and elementary science are regarded not as extras but as basic subjects in all our schools;*
>
> (iii) *until the Asiatic parent is prepared to exercise the self-sacrifice, economy and patience which most Europeans have to exercise if they desire their children to devote several unpaid years to the study of a profession.*

The report also chastises locals for not availing themselves of evening classes in Maths, Physics, Chemistry and Mechanics which were available at Raffles Institution since 1922 and on building construction and design at the YMCA. It concludes the standard of English proficiency of a technical apprentice is not up to the standard of a clerk. Nevertheless, the report recommends that demand for evening classes be fostered more aggressively by employers, noting that the evening Nautical classes were successfully run in Malay.

Regarding trade schools, the report notes that there were very few trades per se, except for the municipal technical departments, the Harbour Board and the Central Engine Works. It further notes that employment opportunities were ethnic and clan-based, that there was no common lingua franca yet and, rather sweepingly, that local boys had an aversion to manual crafts.

Winstedt concludes that they should await an assessment of the Kuala Lumpur Trade School first before throwing any public money at a similar school in Singapore, yet recognizes that Singapore offers, "beyond dispute", the largest scope for mechanical trades of any place in the Peninsula.

Instead, the report suggests that it would be more feasible to "bring manual crafts to the boy than to lead the boy to a trade school". The report strongly advocated that all secondary vernacular schools should have manual subjects made an integral part of the curriculum. It also recommended that the Education Department employs a Chief Instructor at a sufficiently high pay and grade to implement this. This would lead to the "thinking hand" and the foundation of all technical training in Singapore.

Interestingly, the report makes some observations of the link between technical training and unemployment. First, that unemployment was not caused by economic depression or a slowdown in trade, but rather the island's prosperity and rapid development which brought a crowd of immigrants. Hence technical education per se would not lead to any improvement in the unemployment situation, if there were no jobs for such people. Rather, the training would help the locally born to compete with a trained person coming from overseas, a precept that is finding new support in Singapore in the early 21st century. It gives the example that trade schools producing competent motorcar-drivers do not increase the demand for motorcar-drivers, which is a function of economic development.

The report concludes that while the time was not ripe for any specialized technical schools or even trade schools, manual subjects should be incorporated as part of the everyday curriculum of secondary schools, whether in English, Malay or Chinese.

Whether anything came out of the Winstedt Report is not clear, but a Government Trade School was finally opened in 1929 on Scotts Road near Newton Circus.

But suggesting that there was very little other follow up, a further study on Vocational Education was commissioned in 1937. This was a wide-ranging report by H.R. Cheeseman of the Malayan Educational Service with a comprehensive study of Britain as well as schools in Jakarta and Bandung run by the Dutch government.

The Report contained many proposals some of which were followed up. The main recommendations were:

(a) To increase the number of trade schools;
(b) To introduce workshop crafts for boys and domestic science for girls;
(c) To introduce science in secondary schools;
(d) To appoint an overall Organizer for Vocational Education.

The Cheeseman report deviated from the Winstedt Report in many aspects. For one thing, it clearly links training to better employment prospects and career growth. It also promoted the study of hands-on skills for both boys and girls in school, the introduction of science in secondary schools as well as the notion of evening vocational classes for workers.

Certainly, the Catholic Mission in Singapore recognized the need for vocational training when, in 1938, the St Joseph's Trade School was opened. Shortly thereafter, a new building in Balestier was approved by the Government and building works commenced for the Government Trade School. Although completed in 1940, the ongoing war in Europe meant that it was used for the training of military personnel.

When the war reached Southeast Asia, all plans were put on hold until the Japanese surrender in 1945, and the rebuilding of Singapore could start afresh. But this time, the political situation and outlook had changed and a nascent independence movement had begun to take shape.

The pre-war colonial period therefore was a period of vacillation and many committees studying the need for some form of technical education in the colony, with each one making weak recommendations that needed another new committee to look into. An exception was the Cheesman report, which was far-ranging and decisive; unfortunately, the approaching war put paid to most of its recommendations.

The Period of Local Awakening

After the war ended, and the British returned to a badly damaged colony and economy, it was clear that nothing would be the same again. The local population had seen and experienced things that would affect them profoundly. They had seen an Asian power defeat the colonialists, and even worse, they had seen the British and its allies abandoning the colony without much of a fight. The toughest battles were fought by the Malay regiment, suffering huge losses. They had observed how British families were evacuated quickly and how military leaders capitulated under pressure. Local representation in government gradually became more evident in the Legislative Assembly, albeit by nomination of the Governor.

As political consciousness took root, trade and the economy recovered and grew. Technical and vocational education also expanded, driven by the private sector. A number of schools — the Geylang Craft Centre, the Malay Craft School, the Commercial and Industrial School, the Maris Stella Vocational School and the Chinese Girls' Vocational School — appeared on the scene. These were fairly basic in their level of training and fields. For girls, it was limited to the skills of cooking, sewing and housekeeping. The trade school in Balestier became the Junior Technical School in 1951, with about 700 students enrolled in technical courses in the evening. About a fifth of them sat for the UK City and Guilds examination, and more than half did not make it.

Notwithstanding these developments, the emphasis in school education remained on the academic track. The level of industry was small compared to the mercantile and commercial activity in Singapore. Office and clerical skills were deemed to be more in demand than other skills. Education was a diverse activity, with government English schools and a plethora of vernacular schools.

The entrepot trade that Singapore was famous for started to come under the pressure of protective tariffs by Malaya and Indonesia which had begun to industrialize. Furthermore, as primary-producing countries, they began to negotiate direct trade pacts to bypass Singapore as an entrepot hub.

Local businessmen as well as the authorities themselves realized that Singapore had to diversify its economy and industrialize. The shortage of skilled and trained workers began to be apparent. In late 1948, a group of businessmen proposed a British-style polytechnic to train craftsmen and technicians. But the government did not bite. In August 1951, the Singapore branch of the Technical Association of Malaya called for a meeting of interested businesspeople to revive the idea. An ad-hoc committee was formed under educationist and member of the Legislative Assembly, Thio Chan Bee.

The Committee submitted its report to the Governor Sir John Nicoll on 6 September, 1952, recommending a fully equipped and staffed Polytechnic to meet the rapidly growing and urgent needs of the colony for properly trained men and women.

Once again, the British needed another committee, this time headed by Professor EHG Dobby, to make detailed recommendations. The Dobby Report, as it came to be known, was presented in September 1953, a year after the Thio report. The "Report of the Committee on a Polytechnic Institute for Singapore" was a landmark report and can be said to be the first major and significant milestone in the development of technical education in Singapore. The Committee, comprising business and government representatives, made a compelling case for strong government intervention and investment in technical education, using surveys of supply and demand. One key observation was that many European managers and engineers in Singapore were returning home in view of the uncertain local situation and improving prospects at home.

To address the issue that industrial work may not be attractive to local youths, Dobby's solution was to establish a reputable training institution of quality and standards, leading directly to good jobs and promotions. In addition to full-time courses, Dobby had the foresight to recommend a range of courses to upgrade those already in the workforce though evening study. This would help replace the weak and less-than-effective apprenticeship schemes which were the norm then.

The Dobby Report was accepted in principle by the Colonial government and Sir John Nicoll invited AW Gibson, principal of a polytechnic in the UK, to make more detailed recommendations. The Gibson report was very specific in the departments and courses to be offered, the priorities and even the location. He presented his 19-page report in May 1954. The Singapore Polytechnic was established in October 1954 as an autonomous body with its own Board of Governors, but with the government financing the project and operating costs. The first Chairman, Lionel Cresson, a prominent businessman and industrialist, went on a study trip to Britain and Europe to familiarize himself with technical education.

The first Principal DJ Williams was appointed from the UK, and started work in 1956. Architects and Engineers Swan & Maclaren were appointed to design the building (still standing today at Prince Edward Road). Meanwhile, classes were ongoing in different schools and locations even as construction was in progress. In September 1958, when registration at the campus opened, 2800 students, both full-time and part-time, were enrolled for 58 courses in five departments. Dobby's confidence in the demand for hands-on education and his prescience in supporting the establishment of Singapore Polytechnic was spot on.

It had taken numerous commissions, committees and reports over several decades to get to this point. The speed of decision-making only gathered momentum after the war, with increasing and louder local voices and representation. The colonial government was cautious and deleterious in taking vocational education initiatives, reflecting perhaps the class attitudes of the home country. On the other hand, academically outstanding local students had access to scholarships to the best universities in England and to Raffles College locally.

A Joint Advisory Council (JAC) for Apprenticeship Training was established in 1956 as a tripartite council to regulate apprenticeship training. The JAC was only partially successful, primarily in the transport related sectors of ship-repairing, and air and motor transport. In the industrial sectors such as building trades and electrical and mechanical industries, progress had been slow. There was no standardization of apprenticeship schemes across sectors, in matters of duration of training, allowances and supervision.

Technical Secondary Schools

1956 also saw the opening of the first two secondary technical schools (STS) in Singapore, Tanjong Katong and Queenstown. These two schools were the precursors and models for a number of similar schools in the 1960's the offered technical subjects and workshop practice in addition to the usual academic subjects. However, equipment-wise they were deficient until the local government took control of education much later. In his speech day address in 1964, the Principal of Queenstown STS remarked, "As you know this school was called a Technical school only in name till about 1960 as it did not have all the necessary equipment; now I am happy to say that we are well-equipped and I wish to thank the Government for all the necessary funds for the equipment, tools and materials".

It must be noted that at these technical schools (Queenstown & Tanjong Katong and the few others which came on-stream later), the technical curricula offered were not vocational in nature, but considered part of general education. Pupils at Queenstown and Tanjong Katong Technical Secondary Schools also sat for the GCE examinations, but of the University of London Extension Board instead of the Cambridge Examinations Board. Besides Queenstown and Tanjong Katong, the other Technical Secondary Schools that came later were Dunearn Tech, Tanglin Tech, Balestier Tech and Kim Seng Tech.

The Self-governing Period and Merger

The official opening of Singapore Polytechnic on 24 February 1959 by HRH Prince Philip, Duke of Edinburgh, was one of the last acts of the colonial government, for in May of the same year, the first general election where all the seats were completely determined by voters in accordance with the new Singapore constitution was held. The People's Action Party (PAP) won 43 of the 51 seats to form the government. Under the new constitution, full self-government was granted to Singapore, with power over education matters coming under the local authorities for the first time.

One of the priorities of the new government in 1959 was to tackle the high unemployment in the state, with about 30,000 additional young people entering the job market each year. The entrepot economy by itself would not be able to provide the necessary jobs to meet this demand, so the focus of the economy had to shift to the job-creating manufacturing industry. More unskilled workers as well as skilled craftsmen, technicians and engineers were needed quickly.

One institution which saw an immediate change of direction was the recently officially-opened Singapore Polytechnic. In August 1959, a new Board was appointed with Dr Toh Chin Chye as Chairman. Dr Toh was also, notably, the Chairman of the ruling party that took power in June of that year as well as Deputy Prime Minister. The new direction laid out for SP by the new Board was that greater emphasis should be placed on the training of technical personnel. As a result, the following changes were made:

(a) All courses which were available elsewhere were dropped as well as those with small enrolments;
(b) External certifications were replaced with internal examinations leading to the award of Diploma;
(c) The number of departments was reduced by closing the commercial and general education departments.

The emphasis was quickly changed from providing training for white-collar jobs to blue-collar jobs. Typing and stenography courses were closed as were those leading to academic qualifications like GCE and HSC examinations. The internal system of examinations and accreditation was of great benefit to the Chinese-stream students.

Dr Toh further felt that the polytechnic should focus on training of school-leavers and full-time students to prepare them for the job market, not those who were already in some employment, such as apprentices on day-release or evening courses.

The urgent reform of technical education was necessary as the government was in a heated intra-party battle between the democratic socialist wing and the communist-inspired left wing. If the economic and industrial strategies did not work and more young people became unemployed or unemployable, the streets would see more and more violence and clashes.

Between 1963 and 1965, Singapore became a state within Malaysia. The initial euphoria of merger turned however into racial and religious turmoil. It was after the momentous events of separation in August 1965 that Singapore began to chart its destiny on its own. The two years of experiment of being part of a larger national entity was marked by federal–state tensions at different levels. The logic of geography, history, economics and family ties were not enough to keep these tensions creative and constructive. Instead, they took a destructive direction and Singapore became a reluctant nation, not with tears of joy but of sadness.

However, the sudden and involuntary independence translated to determination and resilience, a will to show the powers that be that Singapore could stand on its own and make its own future. Even with a bleak outlook ahead, the adrenalin of independence began to flow in the bloodstream of its leaders and people, and education would be among the new nation's priorities.

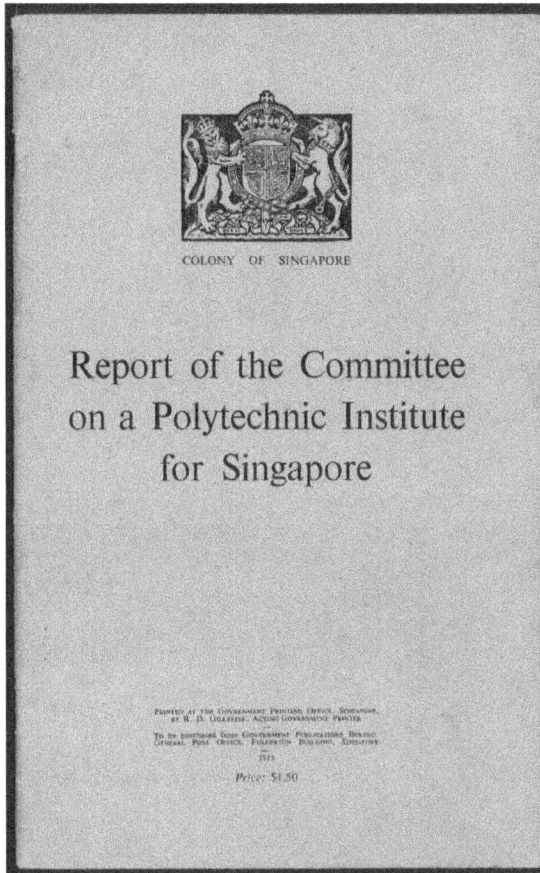

The 56 page Dobby report (1953), one of the documents that outlined the proposal of the setting up of the Singapore Polytechnic.

Prince Philip being shown around the facilities and mingling with the staff and students at the brand new Prince Edward Campus.

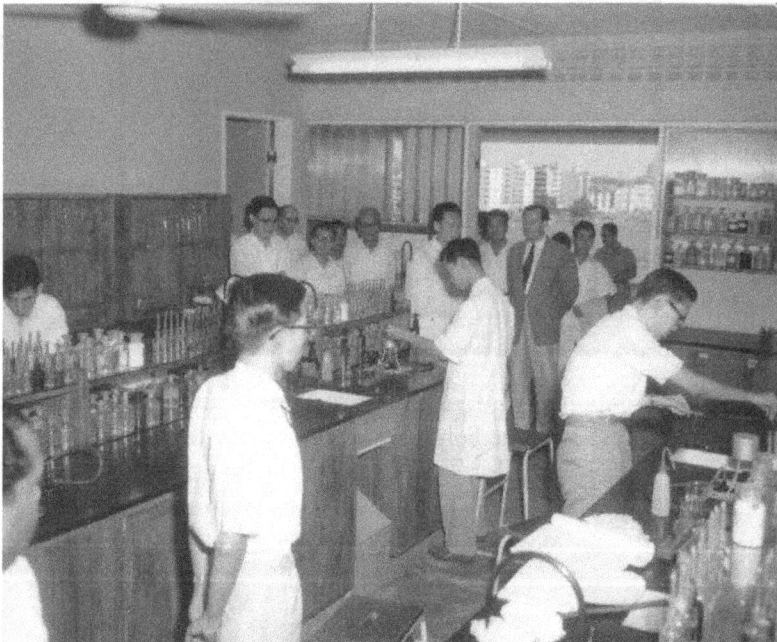

Facilities at the Prince Edward Road Campus.

The Teochew Building at 97 Tank Road was where Ngee Ann Polytechnic first started as a College in 1963.

CHAPTER 2

The Adrenalin of Independence

Landmark Events:

1960: Adult Education Board (Lembaga Gerakan Pelajaran Dewasa) established

1961: Formation of Economic Development Board

1961: Commission of Enquiry into Vocational and Technical Education

1962: Foundation stone of National Iron and Steel Mills laid at Jurong Industrial Estate

1963: Singapore Vocational Institute (SVI) established

1968: National Industrial Training Council (NITC) established

1968: Technical Education Department established in MOE

1969: Singapore Technical Institute established

1969: Baharuddin Vocational Institute for Applied Arts established

1972: Closure of National Industrial Training Council

The 50 years in the title of the book begins with the involuntary granting of full sovereignty to the island state of Singapore in 1965, after two turbulent years as part of Malaysia. Faced with high unemployment, general poverty, poor housing, limited government reserves, a high proportion of under-16's in the population, a high rate of population growth, hardly any natural resources to speak of and dependent on the outside world for fuel and water, it was not a very propitious start to a new nation.

Describing the scenario at independence as dire would be an understatement. At the stroke of a pen, Singapore lost its Malaysian hinterland for its fledgling manufacturing industry, which in any case comprised low technology, low value products. The industrial strategy of the day in all newly independent countries was that of import-substitution, to reduce imports from their former colonial masters and to process and produce basic items in-country for the domestic market.

The aim was to reduce imports of foreign goods and reduce the outflow of foreign currency, while creating jobs for the local population.

With Malaysia and Indonesia going this way, the impact of the entrepot trade would also be significant. With hardly any domestic market, declining port activity, and a heavy dependence on the employment provided by the British military bases, the future looked bleak indeed. Added to this was the diverse population comprising Malays, Chinese and Indians as well as Eurasians, Europeans and the straits-born Peranakans, all speaking different languages and dialects and who, as recently as 1964, had experienced ethnic strife.

Finally, the post-war baby boom meant that about two-thirds of the population was young, below the age of 21. Unemployment was high as there was no indigenous industry worth mentioning, except for commerce, transshipment and the military bases. The literacy rate was just 57% and the majority of professionals and graduates were not from the technical disciplines, but in the arts and pure sciences.

In July 1967, the British government announced that as a cost-cutting measure, they would be closing the British bases in Singapore in two phases. Direct employment in these bases numbered about 30,000, with an even larger number depending on the services provided to the military personnel, including domestic servants, retailers, landlords, provision suppliers, restaurants and so on. 25% of Singapore's GDP was estimated to be generated by the British presence.

However, Singapore in 1965 had three redeeming advantages — a fine deep-water natural harbor, a great location and, most important of all, a team of rational decision-makers who were not afraid to tackle each and every problem systematically and from first principles.

Rapid Industrialisation

The stage was set for a fast-track job creation strategy through rapid industrialisation. The door was opened for multi-national companies to set up operations in Singapore, with plenty of incentives thrown in to attract them. A site in Jurong, in the west of the island, comprising hills and marshes, was identified as Singapore's first industrial estate to house these new entries. To show its commitment, the government opened the first factory there, the National Iron and Steel Mills.

More than an industrial estate, Jurong was developed as an integrated township, with apartments, schools, parks, transport hubs, leisure attractions, shopping centres, food courts, swimming pools and sports venues. After some initial doubts about its viability, Jurong became the model for similar industrial estates in Singapore. With a port, adequate and reliable power supply, roads and telecommunications, and good water supply, Jurong was the symbol of Singapore's resilience and boldness of vision.

Three thousand hectares of industrial land became 6000 hectares. By 1972, there were more than 400 factories operating there, and a similar number in the other 13 industrial estates in other parts of Singapore, many of which were high-rise flatted factories as well as custom-built facilities for multi-national companies (MNCs).

What mattered to technical education was the decision to industrialise rapidly to create employment quickly. Since there was no domestic market for import-substitution, the only alternative was to manufacture for export. This meant inviting, persuading and incentivising MNCs to set up their factories in Singapore.

While good leadership, far-sighted vision and problem-solving acumen were key ingredients to the success of the industrialization policy, the provision of adequately trained manpower was also a key factor in its success. Initially, the process was reactive and to some extent, experimental. Over time, a structure began to emerge, though changing dynamically as the pace of industrialization and the technical skill levels improved over time. The widely-acknowledged economic miracle was built on the foundation of vocational and technical education and educators as well as the administrators who responded equally to the challenges put to them.

Report of the Commission of Enquiry into Vocational and Technical Education

One can trace the development of Technical and Vocational Education and Training (TVET) in independent Singapore to the Report of the Commission of Enquiry into Vocational and Technical Education, or the Chan Chieu Kiat Report, tabled in June 1961. Chan Chieu Kiat was the Principal of Queenstown Secondary Technical School, and prior to this, he had headed a team to study the TVET system in Israel.

The Commission's report was a seminal one, and had a profound impact on the technical training system in Singapore. It described the prevailing situation clearly and the way forward, laying out the future structure of TVET, the role of Singapore Polytechnic, of the school system in preparing for the oncoming force of industrialization, and issues regarding recruitment and training of technical teachers.

In its thorough survey of existing in-service training opportunities in companies, the Commission observed that hardly any instruction took place, and that the apprentice learnt primarily by observing and repeating the job. Secondly, unless the trainee was a relative, the craftsman had no interest in doing the training. Thirdly, as the craftsman himself learnt the trade the hard way, there was no knowledge or science being passed on.

The Commission's report noted that apprenticeship schemes had not been very popular, and that apprenticeship places should be excess to the normal man-power requirements of a company. The government agreed with this recommendation for its own technical services.

The Commission also noted that the two technical secondary schools, Tanjong Katong and Queenstown, were not preparing students for any trade or craft but merely adding some technical subjects like woodwork and metalwork into an academic curriculum; furthermore their school-leavers were pursuing pre-university classes with students from academic schools.

Unlike the technical secondary schools, the vocational schools catered mainly for those who could not complete their Primary School Leaving Examinations, or PSLE. These vocational schools, as we will see later in this chapter, merged with their counterpart secondary academic schools to become bilateral schools and came under the portfolio of the Technical Education Department. Some notable bilateral schools, which naturally had large enrolments, were New Town Secondary, Dunearn Secondary and Thomson Secondary.

Looking at the six vocational and trade schools, the Commission recommended that the Balestier Trade School be upgraded to a Vocational Institute, while the other five operated as secondary vocational schools. These were the first steps to formalize and incorporate technical education into the school system.

First Vocational Institute Established

In 1963, Balestier Junior Technical School became the Singapore Vocational Institute (SVI), the first dedicated vocational institute teaching craft subjects.

In line with the Chan Commission recommendations, the SVI had all the two-year craft courses transferred to it from the Singapore Polytechnic. School-leavers with at least 2 years of secondary education, but who were not academically inclined to progress to the O-level examinations, could take these courses which were in the areas of plumbing, carpentry, refrigeration, air-conditioning, motor mechanics, building trades and so on.

The five secondary vocational schools offered a two-year post-primary course of study in various crafts, feeding into SVI upon completion.

This move also clarified the role of Singapore Polytechnic, which had been offering a plethora of courses at craft, technician and professional levels. With the transfer of the craft courses to SVI, space was created for the expansion of the technical level courses, as the level of knowledge and skills demanded continued to grow. The transfer also allowed for the increase of full-time enrolment and courses. The Commission devoted a whole chapter on its study and recommendations to just one institution, Singapore Polytechnic.

Regarding the secondary school structure, the Commission made radical recommendations. It suggested 4 types of secondary schools — academic, technical, commercial and vocational. There would be channels to direct students to different types of schools based on their primary school performance and aptitudes.

The most striking feature of the Commission's recommendations was the proposal to channel 65% of each cohort to the vocational secondary path, 7% to technical, 8% to commercial and only 20% to the academic path. This radical proposal was not implemented by the government, but it illustrated the huge demand that the Commission foresaw for semi-skilled workers. Only the academic, commercial and technical streams would have a four-year secondary programme. The vocational stream would have a 2-year secondary school programme followed by another two years in a vocational institute.

Equally striking was the emphasis given to commercial and administrative training to support business and industry. The proposal to channel 8% of each cohort in this direction suggests that the Commission was also concerned that businesses should have adequately trained people in the supporting roles of administration, bookkeeping and sales.

As a result of this, by 1968, there were 4 types of secondary schools in Singapore — academic, technical, bilateral or multi-purpose and vocational. The technical schools were similar to the academic schools except that 20% of the curriculum time was devoted to workshop practice and technical drawing. The bilateral schools offered both academic and technical options in the same school. A small number of schools also offered the commercial subjects.

The vocational secondary schools received students from primary schools who did not qualify for the other three. They were given 2-year practical training before going to the Singapore Vocational Institute.

In 1968, it must be noted that out of 100 primary school leavers, the majority, or 3 in 4, went to the academic stream, while only 1 in 8 went to the technical stream and 1 in 7 went to the vocational stream. Similarly, out of every 100 secondary school leavers, more than 9 in 10 proceeded to the academic route, while less than 1 in 10 went to the technical or commercial route. Hence the school educational system was still heavily skewed towards the academic route.

To address this preponderance of academic education which was unlikely to meet the demands of the changing economy in Singapore, the National Industrial Training Council (NITC) was formed in April 1968 to spearhead a "crash" programme of skills training and development. By 1968, the industrialization process was well under way and the demand for skilled and semi-skilled workers was increasing quickly. This high-level council, chaired by the Minister for Education, with the Minister for Finance and Minister for Labour as members, was tasked with establishing the policies regarding technical education and industry-training in Singapore and to achieve the projected numbers expeditiously and effectively.

Formation of Technical Education Department (TED) in MOE

In June 1968 also, all the vocational and technical training initiatives at the Ministry of Education were brought under a single department, the Technical Education Department, better known as TED. This centralization brought with it a sense of purpose and urgency to skills development, and set the stage for a number of rapid changes. The TED was given authority over the development of technical secondary education, industrial training and the technical teachers training department at the Teachers' Training College (TTC). The Vocational Guidance Unit within MOE was also transferred to TED in March 1969. TED also took over supervision of bilateral schools mentioned earlier, together with the other technical schools.

TED introduced a radical shift in the secondary school curriculum, requiring all students to take workshop-based subjects in their first two years. These were offered in their own schools if facilities were available or at established, centralised workshops. Boys and 50% of the girls had to do workshop practice and technical drawing while the rest of the girls had to take technical drawing and domestic science. These subjects, once a week for 3 hours, were in addition to their normal school workload. For those who had to go to a centralised workshop, additional time was spent in travelling to these centres.

The perceived benefit of this extra hands-on training for all secondary school students was to introduce manual skills to them and to help them see new possibilities in their future careers based on practical skills rather than academic knowledge alone.

To radically alter the ratio of primary school pupils entering the academic stream, more technical secondary schools were opened, with a 20% technical curriculum. To ensure follow through at a higher level, technical subjects such as metalwork, woodwork and technical drawing were introduced for the first time at the Higher School Certificate (HSC) level. This was to open up options for students in addition to the Singapore Technical Institute (STI) and the two polytechnics.

The TED also oversaw a shift from school-based vocational training to industry-based training. The secondary vocational schools that were unpopular and did not provide marketable skills training were closed, and converted to industry training centres, assigned to the Adult Education Board (AEB) or integrated with nearby schools. Whereas in 1968 there were only three industry training centres, by 1972 there were nine.

While the technical education system in the formal school system is general and the curriculum is not job or market-oriented, the industry training centres were designed to provide accelerated training to meet industry's specific needs. Training in these centres was oriented to satisfy specific industry requirements.

The two-year craft level programme was modularized in 1970 to accommodate the entry educational level of the trainees as well as the type of training and level of skills required.

Finally, the number of vocational institutes was increased with the opening of new VIs in Macpherson and Bukit Merah in addition to the existing three (Balestier, Baharuddin and Jurong). The target was to move towards a more balanced ratio of 2:1 between academic and technical streams. The role of the Vocational Guidance Unit at the Ministry of Education therefore was expanded and became more proactive in going out to schools to preach the benefits of a technical education. Skilled jobs were the selling point. The Unit also arranged placements for in-plant training for graduates of the various institutions of TED. These contacts with industry provided TED with a good sensing mechanism to understand market trends.

TED also took over responsibility for the apprenticeship schemes from the Ministry of Labour. The Hotel and Catering Training Centre was also transferred to TED. The Technical Education Department of the Ministry of Education became the central player in technical and vocation education during this period, setting the stage for the next phase of development.

While this centralization made policy-making under the NITC more expedient, and implementation by TED more efficient, the personnel and finance protocols followed the civil service instruction manuals. Civil servants were making decisions regarding industry requirements without a direct link to these industries themselves. So although the increase in graduate numbers was impressive, from 324 in 1968 to over 4000 in 1972, industry inputs and requirements were not directly fed into the system.

With this expansion, the problem was less on the quantity of craftsmen and technicians produced, but rather the quality of their job performance in industry. This shift to quality was hampered by the fact that in 1969, there was no uniform standard for determining the level of skills attained. Thus TED also had to develop nationally-recognized trade tests and certificates of competency.

All this required teachers and instructors trained in teaching and developing technical subjects. A nucleus of teachers was formed and a system put in place for more teachers to be trained in technical education. This included re-training of some teachers who were already in the profession.

TED also developed a strong outreach programme of talks, exhibitions, and information pamphlets for students and parents to create a greater awareness of vocational and technical education and the jobs that such training would open up. In an era of high unemployment, jobs were an important consideration for school leavers. Travelling exhibitions and talks in schools were used extensively to sell the benefits of a technical education.

During all of this time, vocational and technical education was directed and executed by the Ministry of Education, under the Technical Education Department.

In 1972, with the initial and urgent need to ramp up skills training over, the National Industrial Training Council ceased its existence. Between 1969 and 1971, nine vocational institutes had been created, raising enrolment in vocational education to 3000.

However, one main problem remained. Primary school leavers who were over-aged as well as those who did not progress to the next level of education were entering the job market unskilled in any trade. It was necessary to have at least two years of secondary education to qualify for a vocational institute or industrial training centre. This was a wastage of manpower which took the policy makers some years to realize and rectify.

Adult Education in Singapore

The only other institution that was a player in the TVE space was the Adult Education Board, more fondly known as Lembaga, headquartered in Fort Canning. The Singapore Council for Adult Education was formed in late 1950 as an independent body, comprising associations interested in adult education as well as some prominent people who were dedicated to the cause of adult education. It received an annual grant from the Ministry of Education to conduct basic education, further education classes as well as classes on general topics for adults.

The grants were used to support various organizations to run basic education classes, and these were also run in many rural areas of Singapore such as Ama Keng, Bukit Panjang, Jurong and Serangoon. In 1957, there were almost 13,000 adults studying Basic Education courses and 900 in the Further Education classes. The Council also organized an innovative course on Elementary Law, through 10 weekly talks on the radio, broadcast twice a week, and two full discussion sessions. With the opening of the Cultural Centre at Fort Canning in 1957, the Council was able to offer a range of cultural programmes as well as lectures and seminars.

In April 1960, the Lembaga Gerakan Pelajaran Dewasa (Adult Education Board) was constituted under the Lembaga Ordinance and in May of the same year, it took over the functions and assets of the Singapore Council for Adult Education. The first Board comprised many eminent names such as C.V. Devan Nair (Chairman) and Jek Yuen Thong (Deputy Chairman), as well as representatives from the Ministries of Culture, Labour, Law and Finance, the University of Malaya and Nanyang University, the Teachers' Training College and the trade unions.

By 1964, the Board was organizing Language and Literacy classes in four languages, General Education classes in three languages, evening classes in commercial subjects leading to LCC certification, vocational-type courses and recreational-type courses. These were held in 153 schools, 30 community centres and other institutional buildings.

By the end of its first decade, the AEB was serving about 10,000 mature students in general secondary education, and another 5000 in special vocational classes for overaged students; the latter comprised classes in metalwork, woodwork, basic electricity, electrical fitting, painting, plastering, technical drawing, industrial orientation, tailoring, cookery and dressmaking. It also organized a number of professional-type courses such as kindergarten teacher training, preparation for examinations run by professional bodies such as the Institute of Banking, the then Chartered Institute of Secretaries, Institute of Business Administration, London City and Guilds, and a large number of personal interest courses.

The AEB was instrumental in giving Singaporeans a second chance at literacy and education, and attending Lembaga classes was a source of great pride for knowledge-hungry Singaporeans.

Thus the scenario in the 1970s was that the TED within the Ministry of Education was leading the changes at school level, Singapore Polytechnic was the sole post-secondary institution for diploma and professional education and Lembaga catered to adults who had either missed out on or dropped out of school and were hungry to move ahead leading to certification by various professional bodies. Lembaga also provided enrichment-type courses so that anyone who wanted to study and learn new skills and knowledge out of pure interest could do so.

It was evident that there was heavy duplication of courses, but without the measurable outcomes that are part of a rigorous skills certification system. These gaps augured the next stage of development in technical education in Singapore.

Baharuddin Vocational Institute was opened in 1969.

In 1969, the Singapore Technical Institute was established to teach students technical skills needed for the new industries that were being set up in Singapore. Located at Circuit Road, the building was renamed ITE MacPherson in 1992. It was later upgraded and reopened in 2002 as the tenth and final satellite campus.

Singapore Technical Institute was established in 1969.

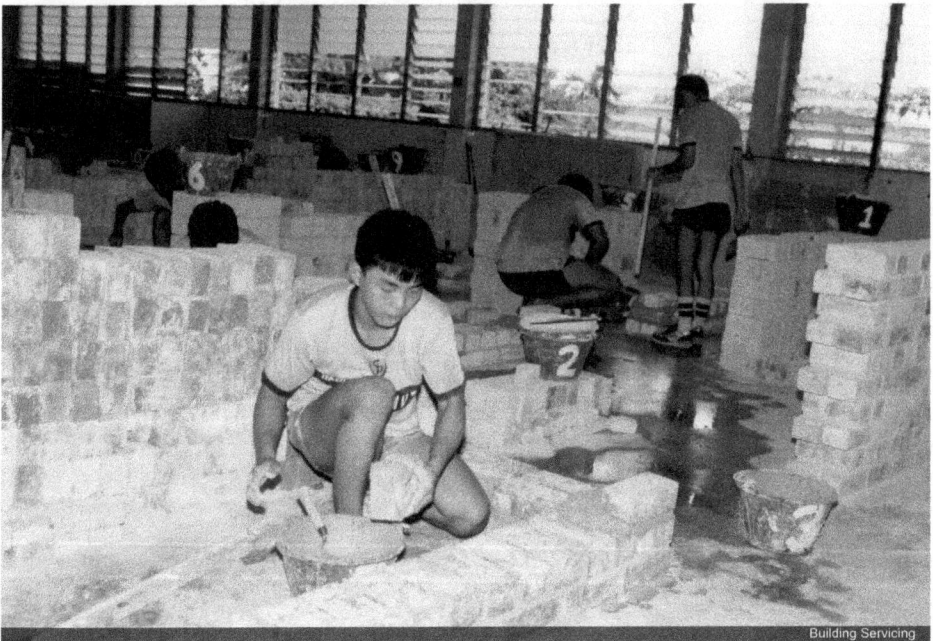

Building Servicing class at VITB to serve the needs of the growing construction industry.

CHAPTER 3

Vocational Training Takes Off

Landmark Events:

1973: Formation of the Industrial Training Board (ITB)
1976: Shelley Report on Review of Technical Education in Secondary Schools
1979: The Report on the Ministry of Education (the Goh Report)
1979: Formation of Vocational and Industrial Training Board
1979: Establishment of Skills Development Fund (SDF)

In Chapter 2, we noted that in 1968, about 3 in 4 of the primary school leavers and 9 in 10 of the secondary school leavers progressed along the academic path. This overwhelming imbalance in favour of the academic path was not aligned with the job-creation-through-industrialisation strategy. The plan would face a skill shortage if this imbalance was not addressed. Hence a National Industrial Training Council was formed that year and the Ministry of Education was organised into two departments, one for general education and one for technical education.

The target to increase the proportion of pupils in the technical stream to 1 in 4 was achieved in stages by reforming the education system, providing the school facilities and training more technical teachers. By 1972, the target had been reached. The number of technical secondary school students swelled from 1600 in 1968 to 7000 in 1972. The target was then moved to 1: 3 or 12,000 students.

By this time, the Technical Education Department had expanded its scope beyond the school system, to include industry training centres, modular training systems, day-release and block-release systems, regulation of apprenticeships, the Singapore Technical Institute and phased intakes, in addition to being the national skills standards body.

Formation of the Industrial Training Board (ITB)

To grow further and to take vocational and technical education to the next level, it was recognised that it was necessary for TED to have more autonomy, greater decision-making power and flexibility. This was done by creating a new statutory board, the Industrial Training Board (ITB). In the case of a statutory board, the government appoints the Chairman and its member and provides it with a charter and an annual budget, and delegates it to meet its mission and goals.

The ITB took its place among Singapore's statutory boards in 1973, taking over the functions and assets of the Technical Education Department of the Ministry of Education while remaining under the purview of the same ministry. As a statutory board, it had the power to determine its own scheme of service, develop its own strategies, recruit its own staff and allocate resources as it saw fit, subject to the supervision of its Board.

The most important development of this change was the strongly tripartite composition of the Board, representing the government, labour (through the unions) and employers. The Chairman was from industry. The Board had its own governance framework with an Establishment committee, a Finance Committee and an ad-hoc Committee on Apprenticeship Training. A major initiative was the establishment of eight Trade Advisory Committees in a variety of trades to provide a more direct relationship between the training provided and the skills needed by these trades. The active and deep involvement of industry in determining the scale and scope of vocational and technical training has become a landmark of the technical training landscape today, and has strengthened rather than weakened.

The establishment of the ITB at this critical juncture of Singapore's development was one of the landmark developments and set the stage for the rest of the 1970's, building the foundation of Singapore's VTE sector for many decades to come.

Those functions of the old TED which related to industrial training, including the institutions and establishments and their staff, were transferred to the new Board. Other functions which were related to technical education within the school system, including the institutions and their staff, were merged with the General Education Department of the Ministry of Education. Thirteen establishments, of which 8 were engineering institutes, were transferred in this manner to the ITB. Among the 13 transferred were the School of Printing, the Hotel and Catering Training School, the Singapore Technical Institute and the Boys' Town Vocational Institute.

The technical teacher training department, which was also under the old TED, became part of the Institute of Education. TED was dissolved, having successfully laid the foundations of technical education and industrial training in the five years of its short but productive existence.

The establishment of the ITB marked the progress which had been made in developing basic skills and craft training. For the next stage of development, of higher order skills in more advanced technologies, a more focussed and more responsive approach was needed. Hence the statutory board model was the preferred option, giving the ITB greater powers and autonomy than the old TED. By placing the ITB in the industry frame of reference, with the various trade advisory committees, the next phase of growth was clearly laid out.

One of the first tasks of the new Board was to determine a new scheme of service for its staff which was attractive enough to support its expansion plans. Once outside the civil service, the Board was less constrained by the civil service schemes which were uniform across the whole service. The other main priority of the Board was the development of more training capacity, through workshops, equipment and classrooms.

The Board, in its very first year of operation, made some key decisions. The first was that the principal vehicle for skills training to the craftsman level would be the apprenticeship system, wherever possible. Secondly, the Board also determined that the basic training programme should be the Trade Certificate course. This was the provision of a sound, broad-based foundation of theoretical knowledge and basic skills in each major trade area, so that the graduates would be suitably prepared for further upgrading as full craftsmen on the job and through apprenticeship.

The National Trade Test System

One of the other key initiatives was putting in place a National Trade Test system, so that there was a uniform system of skill recognition and certification. Certificates were awarded at three levels: a craftsman (Grade 3), a technician (Grade 2), and a master craftsman (Grade 1). The technician Grade 2 certification was awarded on completion of the apprenticeship programme. This three level technician certification remains the basis of later certification systems as these continue to evolve over time to meet new needs and better entry qualifications.

The apprenticeship scheme was affected by the National Service requirement for males to undergo two and a half years of full-time military service. Those who came out of NS were unwilling to go through an apprenticeship programme with an employer. To emphasise the importance of apprenticeship, the government agreed to grant a deferment of NS for those who were on an ITB-approved apprenticeship programme in an essential and critical trade and where ex-NS men could not be recruited. To encourage ex-NS men to take up such apprenticeships, the ITB even introduced an allowance scheme to top-up their apprenticeship allowances. And where a deferred person stayed with the same employer for six years, the government decided not to enlist this person for full-time national service but for part-time duty instead. Such support for industrial training by the government sent very strong signals to the general population as well as school-leavers on the importance of an industry-based technical education.

A major revamp by ITB was to focus more on industry-relevant and industry-specific training. Facilities and resources were reallocated away from the general training of school-leavers to training for specific companies or industries. The strategy was to encourage companies to sponsor students for vocational training, and to take them up as apprentices at the beginning of the training and not at the end of it. One outcome of this was the establishment of industry-specific training schemes, such as the ITB-HDB Scheme for the construction trades where trainees would spend 4 days a week at a Housing Development Board construction site, and 2 days at the Punggol Vocational Institute.

This development led naturally to the one of the most successful innovations and initiatives of the ITB, namely the establishment of Joint Training Centres with companies, with the government sharing the costs. The arrangement was that the joint training centre would train double the number required by the company, freeing the additional trainees to join other companies. The first of these was the Tata-Government Training Centre in 1972, followed by the Rollei-Government Training Centre in 1973. These were located at premises of the vocational institutes. These joint training centres were managed through the Economic Development Board. More of these will be highlighted in Chapter 4.

The Shelley Report — Changing the face of Technical Secondary Education

In 1976, a seven-man committee, led by Rex Shelley, the renowned author, was formed by the Ministry of Education to review the technical education curriculum in secondary schools. Shelley was at that time the Planning Manager for Hume Industries (Far East) Ltd. This was also the period where all male students and half of the female students had to take two technical subjects in their first two years of secondary school. For many of them, the facilities to take these subjects in their own schools were not available and they had to go to centralised workshops, incurring additional travel time.

Given also that at that time, only 16% of secondary school leavers entered the two polytechnics and post-secondary education, the Committee did not feel any need to tailor secondary education towards achieving a better curriculum fit for tertiary education. Eighty-four percent of those completing secondary education in 1976 did not study further. This statistic is amazing by the standards of 2015, where more than 95% of the cohort continue into post-secondary education.

Another telling figure was that the drop-out rate at Primary 6 was 40%, with only 60% going to secondary school after their Primary School Leaving Examination. Since there was no technical content in the primary school curriculum, this meant that a very significant number of youth, at the age of 12 or 13, entered the job market with no or few skills to eke out a living. In the future, they would pose a great challenge to employers and manpower planners as to how to upgrade them to operate machines and be more receptive to technological change.

The Committee decided that technical education should primarily be considered an extension of general education, addressing students' application ability, exploratory and practical skills, and innovation. Hence it was not to be seen as preparation for technical or engineering careers exclusively. Its secondary objective was an appreciation for technical skills and respect for manual or blue collar work. This was especially important because of the heavy focus among students on theoretical knowledge and their general weakness at practical application.

The Shelley Report reaffirmed that technical subjects in schools and centralized workshops were merely a part of general education. These were introduced to help give some focus on workshop subjects which required students to use (and "dirty") their hands, though not to any extent of being regarded as vocational skills acquisition. The report noted that the curriculum time being devoted to technical education was limited and insufficient to prepare anyone for any trade. The committee also concluded, after some debate, that while there was value in workshop practice to destroy any prejudice against manual labour, it was not sufficiently physically demanding or "dirty" enough to have that impact.

The committee also noted that only 24% of secondary students went into a technical stream in Secondary 3 and 4. At the end of Secondary 4, they took the Cambridge O-level examinations which is a key milestone for 16-year-olds in Singapore. The link with Cambridge brought details which were foreign to the Singapore environment at that time, demanding higher standards in technical drawing and machine tools than were needed or taught.

As subjects got more specialised, there was more theory-creep during the technical lessons. The report also enumerated several other difficulties and trends that the committee felt were not compatible with the educational goals of technical education.

The Shelley Report made several key recommendations, such as reducing the curriculum time for technical subjects from the existing allocation of 13% to between 6–10%. This was achieved by hiving off topics to other subjects like Mathematics. Moreover, subjects like commercial studies, principles of accounts and technical drawing were deemed to be too specialised.

The report was also critical of the aptitude tests that were used to channel students at the end of Secondary 2 to the technical stream in Secondary 3, deeming it as imprecise. The aptitude tests were more for mental ability than mental and manual skills combined, resulting in academically bright students being channelled into the technical stream.

The Committee noted that the post-secondary technical institutions admitted students from both the technical streams as well as the academic streams. They saw little advantage accruing to the students in the technical stream. If technical education was to be considered as a further aspect of general education like physical education or music, then by extrapolation, it should be offered to all secondary schools.

As a result of all these considerations, the Committee came to the conclusion that there was no advantage to be gained by continuing with a technical stream in Secondary 3 and 4. Technical education should instead be part of the general curriculum in all secondary schools, spread over 4 years instead of two.

The Committee appears to have had a lot of intense debate internally about technical education for girls. This was not because girls in any way lagged behind boys in skills or speed of learning. They were also convinced that girls were not disadvantaged when it came to physical labour. This was indeed a very progressive position for an all-male committee.

The Committee recognised that there was no longer any societal or cultural prejudice against girls taking up technical education. Indeed, given the demographic trends of declining birth rates, the Committee agreed that such education would help the flow of women into the job market. After some debate, the Committee made a choice between home economics and workshop practice available to girls. Hence the decision was to make technical education a part of the curriculum for girls (with home economics as an option) all the way to Secondary 4, giving gender equality in technical education a boost.

The Committee also recommended that streaming into a separate technical stream was no longer needed as there would no longer be any distinction between academic and technical streams.

Thus ended the story of the secondary technical school system in Singapore. These schools represented the earliest foray of technical education into the formal school system in Singapore, led by the Technical Education Department of the Ministry of Education. It represented the end of an era of rapid growth and experimentation in technical education, trying out different strategies in rapid succession, to get more students to be trained in skills relevant to the growing manufacturing industry in Singapore. But more dramatic changes were just round the corner for the education system as a whole.

Report on the Ministry of Education (the Goh Report)

No study of the history of Singapore's education system will be complete without a study and analysis of the Goh report on the Ministry of Education, for it had consequences for every child in Singapore.

In 1978, Dr Goh Keng Swee, the then Deputy Prime Minister, led a team of non-educationists (popularly known as the system engineers) to study the work of the Ministry of Education. The then Prime Minister Lee Kuan Yew, frustrated with the progress that the Ministry was making, charged Dr Goh to lead a team to study the whole Ministry. There were no terms of reference as such; the membership of the study team was left open and flexible.

Dr Goh selected a handful of scholars and administrators from the civil service with little background in education, who came with a systems viewpoint. They highlighted five key issues to be dealt with, namely high attrition and educational wastage, low outcomes, ineffective bilingualism, and a high variation in school performance which impacted teacher morale on the ground.

What the systems team found was that 65% of the Primary 1 cohort did not successfully complete their secondary education with at least 3 O-level subjects. Furthermore, only 19% of primary school cohorts passed both English and their mother tongue languages at O-level. Comparison of cohort attrition rates with Taiwan and Japan underscored the poor progression rate of the Singapore cohort through the school system.

The Goh team recommended streaming of students to allow different rates of progress for the academically bright and the more average student. The Normal stream was introduced for a 5-year secondary school education with an exit at Secondary 4N and O-levels at Sec 5N. The team was convinced that one system could not do justice to all children, and therefore there should be bridges to correct errors in the streaming process and to accommodate late developers.

With the emphasis on language acquisition in the early school years, and a priority on English (rather than the mother tongue) for the academically weaker students, students who entered vocational or skills training were equipped with an appropriate level of language proficiency from the start. This made skills training more effective in the long run.

It also meant that more students were able to progress to secondary school and complete at least 10 years of education. Later, when the completion rates improved, this set the stage for even more radical improvements to vocational and technical education in Singapore.

Just prior to the Goh Report, there was some tinkering of the school system and curricula at the primary level. Notably there was the introduction of a Basic course at the primary level and pupils in the course were given eight years to complete their primary schooling before they were channelled to the ITB's institutes.

To summarise, the Goh Report (the 'Blue Book') introduced some 'watershed' measures, particularly at the primary level. These included streaming at the end of Primary 3 and the consequential placement of pupils into a monolingual course at Primary 4, the other two courses being the Normal and Extended courses which prepared pupils for the PSLE. Monolingual course school-leavers and those who failed the PSLE were channelled to the ITB/VITB for basic skills training. A new secondary Normal stream for slower pupils was introduced at the secondary level which prepared them for a new N-level examination at the end of their 4th year: those who did well in this examination were allowed an additional year to do the O-level.

With the drop in wastage rates and higher completion rates because of the introduction of more streaming options, more and more pupils were better able to cope with the higher demands of vocational and technical education.

Formation of the Vocational and Industrial Training Board (VITB)

With the expansion of the school system and achievement of universal primary education, courtesy of the work of the TED and later the ITB, the Adult Education Board or Lembaga found the supply of students to its Basic Education programmes dwindling. Similarly, its cultural or personal interest courses were being overtaken by the People's Association with its extensive network of community centres offering similar programmes. It therefore found itself moving into the pre-vocational training for primary school leavers as well as office-based commercial training space. Upon completion of pre-vocational training at the AEB, students were able to enter the craft courses at the ITB.

Hence it was becoming increasingly evident that there would be synergies and economies to be gained by the merger of these two bodies. This led in 1979 to the formation of the Vocational and Industrial Training Board (VITB).

The VITB became an autonomous body and the main provider of vocational and technical training, taking over the functions of the Industrial Training Board and the Adult Education Board (ATB). This was a natural fit, as the AEB (more fondly known then as "Lembaga") had become more involved in pre-vocational and vocational training in its offerings. Initially of course, AEB was meant to be a second chance for adults to complete their GCE O-levels or A-levels. However, it gradually expanded its role over time to offer foundational and vocational courses for young people, in addition to its array of enrichment and cultural offerings for adults.

The merger was made easier because both the ITB and AEB shared the same Chairman, namely Dr Ahmad Mattar, Minister in charge of technical education. In preparation for the merger in 1979, the two boards were also unified, with the ITB Board members taking over the AEB Board with joint Finance and Administration Committees.

The aim of the merger was also to create a single framework for skills training for both students as well as working adults, using common occupational skills standard and tests. These standards were set in consultation with the industry and the trade unions themselves.

From 1979 to 1992, the VITB became the standard-bearer of vocational training in Singapore. The Chairman of the Board was always a cabinet Minister, who was not there in name only, but a very active Chairman, involved in key decision-making and being the bridge between the government and the VITB. Board members were eminent persons, representing government, labour, business and industry.

There were also 13 Trade Advisory Committees (TACs), that were the links with key industry sectors. These TACs were key in the development of the vocational qualifications, the curriculum, the facilities and choice of training equipment.

Skills Certification

The VITB charter included a responsibility to establish skills standards and a system of certification for skills as the national authority for skills certification. The requirements for certification fell into two categories:

(i) Certifying attainment through institutional programmes of training;
(ii) Certifying attainment of skills through continuing education and training, either by attendance at recognized courses, apprenticeship, employment, experience, self-learning or a combination of these.

In an integrated system, the standards and systems of certification for these two routes must be consistent and rational. More important, the qualifications must be acceptable to employers and authorities for licensing of certain trades like electricians and plumbers.

Within the Board, there was a Certification Committee which was also tripartite in composition. The committee comprised the Chairpersons of the Trade Advisory Committees, representatives of the licensing bodies, employer bodies, EDB and standards institutions, and trade unions.

The Certification Committee was responsible for recommending to the main Board the systems of certification; approving the standards of knowledge and skills to be attained; approving the systems of assessment and test plans; and approving the award of certificates to those who successfully passed the assessments and trade tests.

The National Trade Certificate (NTC) was the backbone of the vocational training system. There were three levels of occupational skill certification, as follows:

- NTC-3 indicated basic knowledge and skills of a trade which could be used as a base for becoming a skilled worker. It required 1–2 years of basic training or apprenticeship.
- NTC-2 certified attainment of full knowledge and skill for a specialized occupation or skill. It required 2 years of full-time skills training or 5 years of on-the-job experience.
- NTC-1 was the highest level of attainment, equivalent to a master craftsman or "meister". This was attained after several years of experience and further training.
- Certificates of Competency were for skills that are narrow and specific, usually for artisan trades such as construction, nautical studies and marine engineering.

Intake Levels

The intakes to the VITB came from various levels. With the implementation of the New Education System following the Goh Report of 1978, there were different exit points from school according to academic ability. Hence the VITB had correspondingly different entry points for vocational training for these students.

For the Primary 8 Monolingual (P8M) and Extended (P8E) streams, it was clear to policy-makers that the key to their successful integration into the productive workforce would be through vocational training and education. Hence P8E students were admitted to a Basic Engineering course followed by NTC-3 courses. P8M students were admitted to a pre-vocational training programme after which the better performers would join the P8E in the Basic Engineering and NTC-3 courses. Those who did not make the cut could take up apprenticeship schemes or seek employment under the Junior Trainee scheme.

Those who completed their Certificate in Secondary Education (CSE) could enter directly into an NTC-3 programme or even an NTC-2 programme if their results are good. Those with 2 GCE O-level passes can enter the NTC-2 programme while those with 3 O-level passes can take the higher level 2-year Industrial Technician Certificate (ITC) programme.

In order to ensure that no one remained at a fixed level, there were bridges which allowed trainees to continue to upgrade themselves. For example, NTC-3 holders could proceed to gain an NTC-2 certification.

Skills Development Fund (SDF)

In the mid-seventies, the unemployment situation in Singapore eased as full employment was being reached. The issue then shifted from providing jobs to providing higher value jobs to the limited manpower in Singapore. Not only was there a manpower shortage, there was also a shortage of skilled manpower. There remained in the workforce a very significant number who had not had basic education or training and were paid low wages.

The government, recognising the real possibility of a low-wage trap, created a wage correction policy of raising wages significantly three years in a row. Following the rapid economic growth of the late 1960s and early 1970s, signs of a tight labour market emerged along with a concern that wages might rise without a commensurate rise in productivity. In response, the government in 1972 established the National Wages Council, a tripartite forum with representation from the employers' federations, trade unions, and the government. As a government advisory body, the council recommended annual wage increases for the entire economy, allowing for orderly wage increases and assisting in the development of incentive schemes to improve national productivity.

The wage guidelines were not mandatory but were followed by the public sector (by far the largest employer) and widely implemented in the private sector. The recommendations generally were not applicable to private-sector professional and managerial workers whose wages were determined more by market forces of supply and demand, but was more important for non-professional white-collar and blue-collar workers. Between 1973 and 1979, actual wage increases followed the council-recommended wage increases closely.

In 1979, the government introduced a "wage correction policy", injecting three successive years of high-wage recommendations. This was designed to force an increase in productivity by a structural shift to higher value-added operations, to reduce the reliance on cheap unskilled foreign labour and to raise labour productivity. In tandem with this policy, the government introduced the Skills Development Levy. Every employer was required to contribute 2–4% of its payroll of low-wage workers as a levy to the Skills Development Fund (SDF). The SDF Levy was 2% at the start, rising to 4% in 1982 and then back to 2% in 1985. This was a brilliant strategy as it allowed companies with low-wage workers to use the SDF to upgrade their workers' skills.

The SDF funded the training needs of low wage workers, allowing them to increase their productivity and cross into the high-wage worker bracket. The levy was also an incentive for companies to send their workers for training to gain higher level skills. The Fund also helped to pre-empt redundancies and retrenchments arising from the wage correction policy, by providing companies a way to send their workers for retraining.

The training grant varied from 30% to 70% of the training cost including absentee payroll, approved institutional courses and overseas attachments. Grants were also made to support consultancy for production redesign with related training irrespective of level. The SDF also paid for up to 90% of the set-up costs of in-house training infrastructure, plus assistance for curriculum development, and some recurrent expenditures.

The levy rates have been readjusted over time and today constitutes a rate of just 0.25% of the total payroll of staff earning less than $4500 per month.

Continuing Education and Training

In 1981, a survey by the VITB showed that some 300,000 workers did not possess even primary school education, limiting their potential for upgrading. Hence the

Basic Education for Skills Training (BEST) scheme was launched, offering basic Mathematics and English, in four progressive modules. Successful completion of the four BEST modules was equivalent to a primary school certificate and qualified the holder to take up skills training.

To assist employees upgrading in a modular fashion, VITB also launched Modular Skills Training (MOST), so that companies and employees could develop a very specific training plan, leading to an end-certification that is of use to the company. In addition, VITB also launched Work Improvement through Secondary Education (WISE), for those wishing to improve their English and Mathematics at secondary level.

BEST, MOST and WISE were all eligible for the highest level of SDF grants, or 90% of fees and absentee payroll for employers.

These programmes represented one of the world's most broad-based and integrated education for older workers who missed out on basic education because of the absence of universal education. It enabled them to be more productive, to be upgraded and to become eligible for vocational and technical training with a foundation of mathematics and language. Every mature worker was provided the opportunity to continually better their education and acquire certified skills. Between 1979 and 1991, the VITB trained and certified 112,000 persons, or 9% of the total workforce at that time.

Having done all that, in 1991, VITB launched its Training Initiative for Mature Employees (TIME) in four languages, so that lack of English competency would not be a barrier to education and upgrading.

By the end of the 1990's, the VITB had become the major player in skills development, not only for pre-employment, but also for those in employment. Through a variety of programmes and offerings catering to all levels of literacy and numeracy, VITB created a national ethos of training and upgrading, using in-company resources and its own trainers and facilities. The workforce was gradually upskilled and certified accordingly. Training became more coherent, more easily accessible, and subsidised substantially by the SDF. It must be added that the worker unions, led by the National Trade Union Congress (NTUC), was a key partner with VITB in both facilitating and encouraging workers to be upgraded.

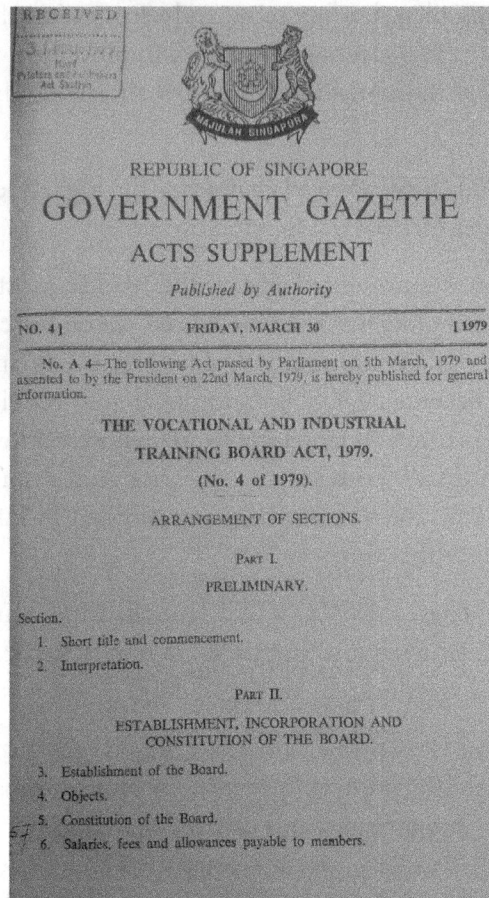

The first page of the Vocational and Industrial Training Board Act, 1979.

Ang Mo Kio Vocational Institute opened alongside nine other Vocational Institutes in the 1980s.

Launch of three-tier National Trade Certificates.

CHAPTER 4

The Role of the Economic Development Board in Technical Education

Job Creation — The Imperative of Industrialisation

The situation that the newly-elected government in 1959 found itself in was truly alarming. The economy was based primarily on entrepot trade and related services. Ships came in to bunker, refuel, get resupplied with provisions, spare parts and so on. Meanwhile their cargo of goods from the major ports of the world would be discharged into godowns or warehouses, for transshipment into regional ports. Then these ships would be reloaded, now with commodities from the region, for shipment back to the industrialised countries for processing.

Another jobs provider was the British naval base, which contributed about 20% of the GDP and supported 30,000 local jobs directly at the base, and indirectly through services to the families of the expatriate servicemen and engineers.

There was little industry or manufacturing to speak of. A large service sector had emerged, both formal and informal, providing the daily needs of the population as well as the professional requirements of the corporates.

The population of Singapore, about 1.5 million at that time, was youthful, with a high birth rate. The government realised that if jobs were not provided fast and soon, a huge social problem would arise, enabling the anti-democratic political forces to exploit the situation and create havoc to bring the elected government down.

Both Malaya and Indonesia, which had achieved their independence from Britain and Holland respectively, had decided on the path of import substitution as their economic strategy, in common with most other newly-emergent countries. This could have a big impact on Singapore's entrepot status as imports to Malaya and Indonesia would gradually decrease. At the same time, both countries embarked on primary processing industries for their raw materials and commodities such as rubber and tin.

Thus the Singapore government embarked on its industrialisation strategy, advised by the Dutch economist Dr Albert Winsemius. The first part of the strategy was to attract foreign multi-nationals to Singapore, bringing with them the technologies, markets and jobs. The attraction for these companies would be low-wages, a package of incentives that included tax holidays, ready industrial land, a nearby deep-water port and good air connectivity. Added to this heady and attractive mix would be a one-stop centre for approvals, cutting of red tape, and an efficient government with zero tolerance for corruption.

From no hinterland, the world would be Singapore's hinterland.

The Economic Development Board

Hence the Economic Development Board or EDB, was formed in 1961 to spearhead the industrialisation process, from attracting overseas investors to providing the local infrastructure such as land, utilities, and roads. Jurong, in the west of Singapore and which was primarily marshland, was identified for the development of the first industrial estate. Hills were levelled, the marshes were filled, roads were built, industrial plots demarcated, flats and schools were built and water and power supplied. Initially the take up was slow. The first factory to start functioning in this barren land was the locally-incorporated and owned National Iron and Steel Mills Ltd.

The foundation stone for the factory was laid in September 1962 by Dr Goh Keng Swee, Minister for Finance and also the man behind the Jurong Industrial Estate. By January 1964, when the official opening was held, production had begun on a commercial scale.

As EDB continued its efforts to bring investors and their factories into Jurong, the industrialisation of Singapore began to take shape. Companies from all over the industrialised world, including Japan, USA and Europe, began operations.

In promising to offer a full-fledged wrap-around service to potential investors as part of its service, EDB found that this included trained manpower. While many assembly operations could be performed by unskilled workers, these operations needed to be supported and supervised by a higher level of technical and engineering knowledge and skills. So while the Industrial Training Board was ramping up its training capacity in a multitude of ways, it was not sufficient to match the needs of the incoming investors, who required customised training.

By virtue of its charter, EDB therefore came to be centrally involved in the development of technical education and training in Singapore and became a key player for the next three decades.

Initially, the EDB's Technical Consultancy Division's Manpower Development Unit focused on management courses to meet the shortage of lower and middle managers to fill the supervisory positions that were being created at great speed. In 1964, all of these courses and programmes were transferred to the newly-established Singapore Institute of Management (SIM). The EDB then proceeded to address the more pressing problem of a shortage of technical manpower.

With the traumatic separation from Malaysia in August 1965, the emphasis shifted from a domestic market to one of export-orientation. This meant a shift in quality upwards, to products that could compete in world markets, using higher technology and a better-skilled workforce.

EDB Training Centres

With the help of the United Nations Development Programme (UNDP), which helped to source technical assistance from countries such as Japan, Britain and France, EDB proceeded to establish six EDB-branded training centres in such areas as woodworking, electro-mechanical and electro-chemical technologies, precision engineering and production prototyping. These came under a new agency called the Engineering Industry Development Agency (EIDA) in 1968.

However, the rate of output of trainees was not outstanding to say the least. Only 86 graduates were produced in four years, after $12 million had been spent. This was not a cost-effective model. However, all of them were immediately employed upon completion of their training. Even more significant was the fact that what had been implanted in these six centres was different training systems from different countries.

MNC-based Training Centres

At the same time, incoming companies were looking for specially trained skilled manpower that was not being produced by the generic training provided by the Technical Education Department or the Industrial Training Board. The companies were also specific about the kinds of equipment and processes which were needed before training could take place.

Hence the next strategy of the EDB was to offer these companies land and buildings to build a training school for their technicians, but with a caveat. This was that the school would also produce an equal number of technicians for other companies in the same industry. EDB offered some capital equipment grants as well as an undertaking to cover 70% of the operating costs. Hence for the companies, they could start their training schools and run them at subsidised costs, while for the EDB, a whole new generation of trainees would be industry-ready, trained in state-of-the art equipment by company instructors.

The training programme was for two years, with one year of basic training and the second on the production floor. Students also received a stipend while in the programme and were awarded an Apprenticeship Certificate on completion. They were bonded to the EDB for five years, and could be posted to any company.

These centres were operated by Tata Precision Industries, then Rollei and Phillips. This was a win-win situation for all: for the MNCs which had access to the specific skills they needed, for the EDB which was able to expand the industry beyond the anchor MNC, and for the student who received not only a training allowance but a good high-skill job at the end of two years of training.

The benefit of being closely involved with MNCs was that the EDB was aware of the exact kinds of skills and personnel needed by the companies, the machinery being used, as well as future plans or changes to existing plans.

By being proactive, and in preparing the skilled manpower requirements while the factories were being built and equipped, the EDB could ensure that the factories would start operations early and create the job growth that was its mandate. In this way, EDB kept its pulse on the supply and demand for skills and manpower as well as the companies' performance.

Fast-track Retraining for British base Employees

The EDB also shouldered much of the training burden caused by the sudden withdrawal of British forces from their bases in Singapore. In 1968, Denis Healey, the British Defence Secretary, announced that the closure of British bases in Singapore would be accelerated, to be completed by 1971.

The withdrawal meant that 38,000 persons would be unemployed, or 20% of the total workforce. In addition, Singapore would see the loss of 25% of its GDP as a result of the loss of spending by the British government, and the troops and their families. Clerical staff, telephonists, cooks, domestic maids, drivers, gardeners as well as the technical staff would all be impacted. Their only hope of re-employment was to acquire marketable technical skills.

In March 1968, a crash training programme was worked out between the EDB and the Ministry of Education. Retraining courses in metalwork, fitting, machining, radio maintenance and plumbing were offered. All available rooms at schools, training centres and vocational institutes were used.

This crash retraining was not an unqualified success in terms of numbers of people trained and redeployed. However, EDB became proficient in quick response and in working closely with other government agencies. This came in useful in 1970, when the Suez Canal was closed by the Egyptian government and ships were re-routed through the Cape of Good Hope, a much longer route. This created a minor boom in Singapore's ship-repair industry caused by the increased wear and tear of the ships as they navigated through rough seas. At the same time, the nascent oil-rig construction industry also experienced a boom from the increase in oil exploration in the South China Sea.

Together, this created a sudden surge in demand for certified welders, for both the ship repair as well as the rig construction industries. Once again, EDB swung into action with its partners, creating facilities for the mass training of welders. Between 1970 and 1973, 1,789 welders were trained through full-time, part-time and ad-hoc short courses, feeding the burgeoning ship-building, repair and oil-rig construction business. These helped Singapore become one of the leading rig-building centres in the world, even without a drop of oil to its name, just as it also became a leading oil-refining centre.

Foreign Government-led Training Centres

From the small EDB training centres and the MNC-led training centres, the next phase of EDB's involvement in technical training was when it led the establishment of institutes of technology, with the financial and technical assistance of foreign governments. This was in response to the government's high-wage policy in 1979, and the establishment of the Council for Professional and Technical Education (CPTE) chaired by the Minister for Trade and Industry.

Following the rapid economic growth of the late 1960s and early 1970s, signs of a tight labour market emerged, along with a concern that wages might escalate. In response, the government in 1972 established the National Wages Council, a tripartite forum with representation from employers, trade unions and the government. As a government advisory body, the council recommended annual wage increases for the entire economy; ensured orderly wage development so as to promote economic and social progress; and made observations and recommendations regarding national productivity.

Between 1973 and 1979, actual wage increases followed the NWC recommended wage increases closely. As mentioned in the previous chapter, in 1979, a "wage correction policy" was announced by the government, in which there were three years of high-wage recommendations.

The implementation of these recommendations and subsequent wage increases meant that Singapore had to move to higher value-added manufacturing and services, and quickly. The CPTE supported the EDB's proposal to establish foreign government funded technical institutes. These institutes would speed up the transfer of knowledge and technology especially in the areas of growth.

The first, the Japan–Singapore Training Centre (JSTC), was opened in 1979. The second institute was the German–Singapore Institute (GSI) funded by $12 million worth of German equipment and $15 million worth of technical expertise in production technology, such as advanced factory automation and computer-aided manufacturing.

In 1982, the Japan–Singapore Institute of Software Technology (JSIST) was established, in anticipation of the growth of the Information and Communication

Technology (ICT) sector, to support the computer software and services industry. Under an agreement signed between the two governments, the Japanese government provided technical assistance through the Japan International Cooperation Agency (JICA). Donations of hardware and software worth $8 million were made by Japanese IT giants as well as 24 training fellowships in Japan to train local lecturers.

This was followed by the French–Singapore Institute (FSI) in 1983, specialising in electro-mechanical and electronics technologies. Providing initial and further training in the fields of electrical and electronic engineering with emphasis on industrial electronics, factory automation and industrial computing, it was established with the support of the École Supérieure d'Ingénieurs en Électronique et Électrotechnique (ESIEE), a reputed "grande écoles" of the Chamber of Commerce and Industry of Paris (CCIP).

These institutes accepted trainees who had completed their A-levels (12 years of education), offering two-year diploma programmes in their respective disciplines. The students put in a 48-week year and 44 hours of training per week, just as long as a normal work day in Singapore.

The training philosophy was to simulate as closely as possible the working environment, under a common pedagogy known as the "Teaching Factory" concept. This was the hallmark of the EDB institutes. They all had very close links with local industry partners, with their respective management boards drawn from leading companies. Both students and lecturers were closely involved in real product and process development, solving industry problems and preparing students for life as they would find it in the workplace,

Being close to industry, EDB continued to develop and fund specialised programmes to meet immediate and projected demands. For example in 1986 and 1987, EDB established a post-graduate programme in integrated circuit (IC) Design and Automation Engineering. Then in 1988 and 1989, four post-diploma programmes in the areas of product design, factory automation, tool and die design and automation were launched. For technicians, a surface mount technology programme was introduced.

Dr Linda Low in her book on the EDB wrote "The greatest innovation that the EDB made in Singapore's industrialisation efforts must, however, be in its manpower and training schemes." This is despite the fact that the EDB has offices world-wide, with its officers always looking out for new trends, new technologies, new business models to bring to Singapore to create good and well-paying jobs. The EDB as a one-stop centre for foreign investors did not leave any stone unturned to make Singapore the preferred destination for inward foreign direct investment. If it meant making the right skills available to a major investor or industry, it did not flinch from doing so.

But those were the heady early days of industrialisation. Today, the educational landscape has changed tremendously. Five polytechnics with 250 diploma programmes, five publicly funded universities, and a world-renowned technical education system of the Institute of Technical Education (ITE) form a formidable foundation for an educated, knowledgeable and skilled society, responding to requirements as they occur.

In the next chapter, we will examine the growth of the polytechnic sector, and the important part it plays in the overall technical education landscape of Singapore.

The Jurong Campus of the French–Singapore Institute.

The Jurong Campus of the German–Singapore Institute.

CHAPTER 5

Polytechnics Come of Age

Landmark Events:

1954: Establishment of Singapore Polytechnic (SP)

1963: Establishment of Ngee Ann College by the Ngee Ann Kongsi

1967: Ngee Ann College comes under the Singapore government

1968: Ngee Ann College becomes Ngee Ann Technical College (NATC)

1976: First Singaporean Principal of SP, Mr Khoo Kay Chai, appointed

1982: NATC renamed as Ngee Ann Polytechnic (NP)

1990: Establishment of Temasek Polytechnic (TP)

1992: Establishment of Nanyang Polytechnic (NYP)

2002: Establishment of Republic Polytechnic (RP)

The Polytechnics in Singapore, today numbering five, play an important supporting role in economic development through the provision of highly-trained para-professionals to fill mid-tier positions in industry, business and services. This positioning of the polytechnics took some decades to come about; in the early days of technical education, Singapore Polytechnic was the only post-secondary institution in Engineering and Technology, covering trade skills, technical education as well as professional education.

Over time, with the establishment of institutions in vocational training and professional education, the role of the polytechnics as the primary providers of mid-tier para-professionals became established. The planning parameter for this was initially 4 para-professionals or diploma holders to each professional or graduate. As the economy went through its evolution to become more capital-driven and then more knowledge-based, this ratio became 2 para-professionals to support one professional. As University enrolments expanded in line with economic growth, the polytechnic sector also aligned and adapted itself. In this chapter, we will see how the polytechnic sector developed to become the linchpin in the growth story.

In Chapter 1, we noted the establishment of Singapore's first polytechnic in 1954 and its official opening amidst much fanfare by HRH the Duke of Edinburgh shortly before the first government was elected in Singapore. With self-government, the whole direction of the polytechnic was changed to one of supporting the new economic policy of rapid employment creation through industrialisation.

New courses in engineering technology were introduced, the trades courses were hived off to the Industrial Training Board (ITB) and the professional diploma courses were transferred to the University of Singapore (SU) as degree programmes. This left Singapore Polytechnic (SP) with the technician diplomas in Mechanical Engineering, Civil Engineering, Electrical Engineering, and the various Certificate of Competencies in Nautical Studies. For many years, the development of SP paralleled Singapore's own development, both economic and social.

When Singapore was declared a sovereign and independent nation on 9 August 1965, her survival depended entirely on her human potential aided by a good geographical location. But apart from these, Singapore had little in terms of land, natural resources, water supply, hinterland or any other aspect that could provide a sound basis for economic development.

The polytechnics in Singapore played and continue to play a central and critical role in the training of the core manpower for Singapore's business and industry. They have evolved over the decades to become powerhouses of global repute, popular among students and employers. This chapter will trace their development, not as individual institutes but as a whole sector in the TVET landscape.

The 1960's — a Period of Change and Consolidation

The initial growth spurt occurred in the 1960's, upon independence. Singapore Polytechnic went through some radical and wrenching changes from a colonial institution to a forward-looking training institution to fuel the planned industrial growth of Singapore into a manufacturing hub. The first of these changes arose from the Chan Chieu Kiat Report when all the craft courses were transferred out to the newly-established Singapore Vocational Institute (SVI), housed temporarily at the Balestier Trade School. This provided the polytechnic with more focus and room to expand its technician level and professional level courses.

For a brief period, upgrading SP to an Advanced College of Technology, follow-ing a similar trend in Britain, was considered. Much preparation went into this proposal, such as a 1964 Colombo Plan study team from Britain led by Dr C A Hart which recommended a relationship with the University of Singapore as the degree-awarding body for polytechnic professional courses in Accountancy, Architecture and Building. The first such graduates were awarded the Accountancy degree in 1967.

To further support this upgrading, staff were sent on scholarships overseas, there were visits by experts from the Ford Foundation and some research schemes were initiated. Staff strength grew from 268 to 338 between 1964 and 1965 alone. Staff were allowed to do consulting work as part of their contracts.

All these came to nought for the Polytechnic, but were a gain for the University of Singapore, for by late 1968, a clear decision was taken after a long debate that the Polytechnic should remain a technician-training institution and not dilute its focus with a mixed mission and mixed staff expectations. The professional courses were transferred together with the staff to the University of Singapore and became the foundation of the three faculties of Engineering, Accountancy, and Architecture and Building. However, for some years yet, the Faculty of Engineering remained at the Polytechnic's premises at Prince Edward Road until the new University campus at Kent Ridge was ready.

While these changes were disruptive for the interim period, especially for students and staff, in the long term, it provided clarity to the polytechnic's mission and created a more sustainable growth path for both institutions in the 1970's and beyond.

SP began to focus on technician training, and started the two-year Industrial Technician Certificate (ITC) course as a bridge between the craft courses of the ITB and the three-year technician diploma. Together with the regular diplomas in the School of Industrial Technology and the Certificate of Competencies (CoC) from the School of Nautical Studies, the student enrolment took off, growing to almost 5400. An annexe building at Prince Edward Road was built, followed by satellite campuses at Ayer Rajah and the Princess Mary Barracks in Dover Road to cope with the increases.

At the same time, there were also tumultuous changes happening at Ngee Ann College, a private university offering four-year degrees. Established as a counterweight to Nanyang University by Chinese businessmen and philanthropists from the Ngee Ann Kongsi (or clan association) representing the Teochews in Singapore, the College began life at the Kongsi's headquarters in Tank Road. Undaunted by staff shortages and declining intakes, the Kongsi made expansion plans for a new campus in Clementi Road where it owned land.

Two leading American educators, Prof Lucien Pye of MIT and Prof Arthur Singer of the Carnegie Foundation, were invited to make recommendations for its growth path. These consultants, after extensive consultations, recommended that the College take the shape of the US-style community college, offering a wide range of technical and professional courses as well as something for worker upgrading and continuing education. Their report, which was accepted by the Kongsi, became the basis of the new campus. However, the building project led to violent protests by students who felt betrayed by this perceived downgrading to technical education. There were also internal rifts within the Board regarding the ability of the Kongsi to finance the project and the running costs of a university, and soon the building construction was halted. When news of this became public, the students demanded the reasons for the halt. On 7 June, 1965, the entire enrolment of a thousand students boycotted classes for two days in protest.

Prior to this, the government itself had commissioned a small panel to study the future of Ngee Ann College. The Thong Saw Pak report, named after the committee Chairman Professor Thong of the University of Malaya, made the far-reaching recommendation that the College should become a public institution to train commercial and industrial technicians at Diploma level. The recommendation was accepted by both the Kongsi and the government and on 7 September 1967, the College went from private to public through the passing of the Ngee Ann College Act in Parliament.

The first Council meeting decreed that as a public institution, all the administrative staff and classes should be moved out of the Kongsi's premises in Tank Road to the new building in Clementi. The turnaround of Ngee Ann College had begun in earnest and with the government taking the lead, quick and fast decisions were possible. In 1968, the government funded the first diploma course in Mechanical Engineering. In the same year, the College changed its name to Ngee Ann Technical College (NATC). By 1971, a diploma in Electrical Engineering and courses in Business Administration and Corporate Secretaryship had been launched. Soon the last students of the degree programmes graduated and those courses closed. Also in 1971, English replaced Chinese as the medium of instruction and in April of that year, NATC welcomed its first batch of non-Chinese students.

Thus, by the end of the 1960's, the character of Singapore Poly and Ngee Ann Technical College had been settled, and this helped to fuel their growth over the next few decades. The industrialisation programme of the government had by then taken off, creating an increasing demand for trained technical manpower.

The 1970's — the First Burst of Growth

In the 1970's, both SP and NATC experienced the first of many growth spurts. Indeed, after the period of change and consolidation in the previous decade, one can say that they never stopped growing and developing. As Singapore moved from a low labour-cost and labour intensive economy to a high-technology and high-skill economy during this period, the demand for skilled and trained technicians continued to be strong.

Singapore Poly, through the intervention of Dr Toh Chin Chye, was able to obtain the site of Queen Mary Barracks in Dover Road, covering an area of 37 hectares and which had been released by the British Army to the Singapore government. In 1975, construction started on a new $53 million planned campus. In 1978, the entire Polytechnic moved from its 3 campuses to its new campus, where it still is today.

At the same time, Ngee Ann Technical College embarked on its own expansion plan on a 20 hectare site donated by the Kongsi. In order to build up its reputation and quality of its diplomas, NATC entered into a long-term relationship with the Polytechnic of Central London (PCL), with three senior staff being seconded over, including the Vice-Principal, the Head of the Electrical and Electronic Engineering Department and the Commerce Department. Between 1975 and 1979, all diplomas were awarded jointly by NATC and PCL.

Ngee Ann's first 5-year phase of expansion began with the official opening of the campus in 1978 and brought it on par with Singapore Poly, as both institutions completed their expansion plans. This coincided well with the economic reconstruction that was happening at the time, phasing out labour-intensive industries with low value added per worker. Many new programmes were added covering the priority areas that were laid out by the Council for Professional and Technical Education (CPTE). With this came an emphasis on higher order technical skills with a focus on computing and design.

The 1980's — the Second Growth Spurt

Even as the 1st phase of expansion was being completed and deployed for training, the CPTE increased its targets for technician output. Both Singapore Poly and Ngee Ann Poly having completed a major upgrading of facilities, were again charged with a 2nd phase of expansion.

As the curricula, courses and standards of both institutions began to converge, given the government's investment in buildings, facilities and equipment, it was a natural next step to standardise the terminology and call them both polytechnics. Hence in 1982, Singapore's second polytechnic, Ngee Ann Polytechnic came into being, at the same time as the 2nd phase of expansion was announced, costing $200 million for Ngee Ann and $182 million for Singapore Polytechnic.

This 2nd phase of expansion for both institutions brought the total capacity of polytechnic education to 18,000 students, with facilities rivalling overseas universities. During this time, the face of polytechnic education began to change. As both institutions became larger in size and enrolments, a more comprehensive range of facilities were provided, such as first-class sports and recreation and arts facilities, student centres, modern libraries with online OPAC and digital resources. Together with this, corporate planning, staff professional development, educational quality assurance, staff recruitment from overseas, and links with like-minded institutions such as the Association of Canadian Community Colleges (ACCC) were established. The international footprint of the polytechnics began to expand as more and more universities came to recognise the quality of polytechnic graduates from Singapore and provided incentives and credit transfers to their degree programmes.

By this time, the range of courses at the two polytechnics had broadened to cover a wide range, including Business Administration, Computer Studies and Software Technology, Accountancy, and a wide range of engineering programmes, including ship-building and offshore engineering, electronics, and architectural drafting and model-making. The emphasis and bias was still on hard engineering courses. By the mid-80's, Singapore Poly could boast the largest CAD/CAM training infrastructure in the world, and all the diploma programmes had a strong element of CAD included.

In 1988, the 3rd phase expansion for Singapore Polytechnic was announced to push the enrolment to 12,000 students. Similarly for Ngee Ann Polytechnic, two more expansion phases were announced in 1990 and 1992.

The 1990's — the 3rd Growth Phase and Greenfield Polytechnics

While both polytechnics were growing rapidly in size, scale and offerings during the 1970's and 1980's, nothing could compare to the growth phase of the 1990's. During this decade alone, the Singapore government announced the establishment of two new full-sized polytechnics; this effectively doubled the national capacity of technician training over just one decade.

The first of these new-generation, greenfield polytechnics was Temasek Polytechnic. Not only was it the first public polytechnic to be built from scratch since 1967 when the government took over Ngee Ann College and converted it to a technical college, it was also the first to be designed from the beginning to accommodate a student enrolment of 12,000. Whereas the earlier polytechnics were expanded in various stages in response to increasing demands to meet the changing economy, here came an opportunity for an outstanding masterplan.

Being the first new polytechnic in more than two decades also offered Temasek Polytechnic the opportunity to organise itself in a new way, with fewer Schools (such as Business, Design, Engineering, IT, Applied Science), instead of many departments, each dedicated to a diploma (for example the Mechanical Engineering department offering a Diploma in Mechanical Engineering, and so on). This new arrangement allowed each School to be able to develop and launch new diploma programmes more expeditiously by combining existing modules as well as modules within its area of discipline. The first such diploma was the Diploma in Mechatronics, combining electronics, control and mechanical engineering. It also made it easier for two or three Schools to collaborate and offer interdisciplinary diplomas, such as a Diploma in Business Information Technology.

The new polytechnic also was a pioneer in creating niche diplomas as well as opening up programmes to fill the rapidly expanding service sector, such as Tourism and Hospitality, Retail Management, Design, Logistics & Operations Management and Apparel Design & Merchandising. A good example of this was the Diploma in Legal Studies, providing trained para-legals to assist lawyers in their work with research and case preparation. This was in anticipation of a generation of law clerks who had learnt their skills on the job, and who were on the cusp of retirement. This was the kind of competitive innovation that the new polytechnic brought to the landscape, creating new disciplines where none existed before, and which were thought to be the purview of the Universities.

Temasek Polytechnic was also the first to create authentic learning environments within the campus. A student-managed retail store, travel agency, restaurant and a hotel room gave students real life experiences and confidence even before entering the job market. The industry-grade facilities include a clean room for making semiconductor chips and performing quality assurance on them, so that students who will work in semiconductor wafer fabrication plants in the future would be at ease with the micro- and nano-scale of the technologies they would have to work with and use. These facilities also created a more holistic learning environment encompassing business planning, budgeting, marketing, accounting, project management, negotiation and presentation skills, as well as the ability to work in a team and manage conflicts.

This laid the foundation for the implementation of problem-based learning (PBL) across all the Schools and programmes. The impetus for PBL came from the realisation that all knowledge and skills taught in any programme faces the risk of obsolescence. Hence what would serve the student best is the skill of analysing and deconstructing a problem, seeking solutions to each part, and to synthesise a solution in the given time frame. This simulates what the graduate would have to do in any workplace any time into the future. It creates a structured self-learning and self-finding approach to knowledge and skills, or just-in-time learning as opposed to just-in-case learning. The mission of the polytechnic was rephrased to "to prepare school-leavers for a future of dynamic change", using innovative pedagogies such as PBL and values-based education, as the anchor for their future.

Temasek Polytechnic also required all academic staff to complete a two-year teacher training programme which was externally accredited. This helped to build the pedagogical muscle for all the innovations that were being created and implemented. For students, a mandatory module of Character Education, a values-education programme, was established which continues to be implemented today.

Building a new campus for 12,000 students (now extended to 15,000 students) was also an opportunity to design a campus that was aesthetically pleasing while being conducive to learning and student interaction. The end result is a campus located beside a reservoir in eastern Singapore that can claim to be the most attractive polytechnic campus in the world. Even though the reservoir is not part of the campus, it is incorporated into its design, using the Japanese concept of "shakkei" or borrowed scenery. Students and staff regularly walk or jog around the reservoir during the morning or evening.

All of these positioned the new kid on the block as a pioneering and innovative polytechnic, much admired and emulated. Over time, all the polytechnics (soon there would be five), adopted many of the organisational and pedagogical innovations that were first implemented at Temasek Polytechnic. The two earlier polytechnics moved towards the School model while the two new polytechnics that came afterwards adopted this same model from the outset.

With the apparent success of Temasek Polytechnic and the high employment rates of polytechnic graduates, the government decided to increase the cohort participation rate in the polytechnics to 40% (of a cohort size of approximately 50,000). This meant places for 20,000 students annually. This participation rate has since increased to 45% to account for the numbers who proceed to degree study at Singapore and overseas universities.

In 1992, barely two years after Temasek Polytechnic's founding, the government established the fourth polytechnic, Nanyang Polytechnic, with a School of Health Sciences as the foundational school, offering diplomas in Occupational Therapy, Nursing, Physiotherapy and Radiography. These diploma programmes were actually included in the recommendations of the 3rd Polytechnic Task Force, but were not approved at that time. However, in the span of two years, new thinking prevailed that there would be benefit from such courses being offered at an educational institution, rather than by the Ministry of Health. Students at a poly-technic would benefit from a wider range of resources and interactions and enjoy a fuller campus life.

The following year, all the EDB training institutes (see Chapter 4) were trans-ferred from the EDB to Nanyang Polytechnic (NYP). The French–Singapore Institute (FSI), German–Singapore Institute (GSI), Japan–Singapore Institute (JSI) and Precision Engineering Institute (PEI) transferred to NYP to form the founda-tions of its School of Engineering. In a single move, NYP became a leading institute of training for factory automation, mechatronics, robotics, as well as communica-tion technologies, having benefitted from the knowledge transfer from leading French, German and Japanese institutions. Under the transfer, the entry require-ments were changed from A-levels to O-levels and the diploma duration extended from 2 years to 3 years. This brought the Institute's programmes in alignment with the rest of the polytechnic sector.

NYP established its niche and specialisation in its "teaching factory" concept. Under this training pedagogy, the laboratories and classes were designed to be as close as possible to an actual work environment. Teaching staff worked very closely with business and industry to bring real-life problems and projects into the polytechnic and students were assigned in groups to create the solutions. The Polytechnic charged market-rates for these projects just as any other company would. Contracts were signed as in the real world on quality, cost and delivery dates.

These projects created a very realistic environment for learning. Both staff and students were challenged and the learning was both deep and multi-dimensional. The projects were of industry quality and would be incorporated into the com-pany's operations. The only issue was cycle time, as it took up to a year to deliver the products.

Nanyang Polytechnic also had a marvellous new campus, master-planned from the start, and was located next to a busy MRT station, providing easy access to students from all over Singapore.

The 2000's — Polytechnics Come of Age

In August 2002, the fifth polytechnic, Republic Polytechnic (RP), was established, with its new campus to be located in northern Singapore. That 3 new full-scale polytechnics of about 12,000 students and 1300 staff each could be established in a period of 12 years demonstrated the depth of management skills available within the polytechnic sector. With each new polytechnic being established, key management staff were identified from other polytechnics and other government agencies to form the key leadership team. Together with a supervisory board comprising industry leaders, all the governance structures could be established quickly and processes put in place.

Recruitment of academic, administrative and support staff then took place and operations usually began in a temporary campus. In the meantime, architects, engineers and project managers were appointed to design and build the new campus according to the specific requirements of the polytechnic. Each polytechnic created its own niche programmes and distinguishing characteristics.

The Republic Poly campus was master-planned and designed by Fumihiko Maki of Japan around an Agora, allowing for student interaction within a circle of identical academic blocks. For its niche area, RP specialises in Sports and Recreation Management as well as the Arts. It is positioned as an Arts hub for the north of Singapore. RP also adopted Problem-Based Learning (PBL) heavily in its initial years as the key pedagogy in all its programmes.

With the five polytechnics, each approaching a student enrolment of 15,000 and catering to a cohort participation rate of 45%, the sector is the key post-secondary path in Singapore. There are now 250 diploma programmes to choose from across all the five polytechnics. Together with the 25% of each cohort going to the Institute of Technical Education (ITE), about 70% of each cohort takes the TVET route to education. However, only about 50% go into hard engineering programmes. TVET now includes a wide variety of service-related careers in areas such as ICT, allied health, business and accounting, sports, retail, tourism and hospitality, and many others.

This has made TVET attractive to female students who comprise at least 50% of the total enrolments of the polytechnics. While engineering enrolments are still 60% male, the large number of services-related courses such as business, accounting and finance, infocomm technology, retail and hospitality, as well as creative courses such as design, media and film-making, have made polytechnics equally attractive to females as well.

All the polytechnics also have strong entrepreneurship development programmes built into the curriculum as well as support systems for new entrepreneurs. This includes finding, refining raw business plans, finding seed and venture capital, mentoring, and even taking equity. Much of these is done through the polytechnic's own alumni who are successful entrepreneurs in their own right.

With their world-class campuses, diverse offerings, and international linkages, the polytechnics in Singapore have come of age in the last 25 years. They innovate constantly, read the market well, and provide market-driven education and training which leads to employment.

Strong Outreach to Schools

Although the Institute of Technical Education (ITE) has three Colleges in its system, it is still organisationally one single entity. The five polytechnics on the other hand, are autonomous entities in their own right, though they all come under the jurisdiction of the Ministry of Education. There exists therefore a strong competitive spirit for students, placements, staff, industry partnerships and honours.

The first of these, the competition for students, has resulted in innovative approaches to secondary schools who are the feeders to the polytechnics. From Open Houses, Parents' Days and competitions for schools held at different polytechnics, to priority admission for star students in sports, arts and academics, the polytechnics try many different approaches to market themselves and their courses to secondary schools. As a result, even with an intake of almost 28,000 students a year, the polytechnics remain a popular choice. This has also resulted in a much better quality of students in the polytechnics, with about four in ten of those who enter the polytechnics being eligible for the more direct academic route to a university degree, that is through the junior college route if they wished to, but preferring the polytechnics instead.

This was not always the case. In the 1980's and 90's, school teachers who had been little exposed to technical education or polytechnic education did not consider polytechnics the first choice for their students. But with high employment rates, good jobs, and a route to a degree opening up for diploma graduates, the career guidance counsellors in schools could not ignore what the students themselves already knew.

Similar strategies have been adopted by ITE in its quest for students and to maintain its quality as well. As we will see in the next chapter, the ITE transformation is a story in itself.

Clarity of Mission

Polytechnics themselves are not unique in other parts of the world. However, they could mean different things in different countries. In Switzerland for example, the Ecole Polytechniques in Zurich and Lausanne are high-end research and teaching institutes at the top end of the technological pyramid. In the United Kingdom, the polytechnics, which offered degrees accredited by the Council of National Academic Awards (CNAA) and diplomas of the former British Technical Education Council (BTEC), were upgraded to autonomous universities in the early 1990's with the goal of delivering mass higher education with a more applied and industry out-look. The same has happened to the Institutes of Technology in Australia.

Only in Canada and the United States have the community colleges main-tained their character and mission, though there is also a clear trend to use the college diploma or associate degree as a direct pathway to university. In developing countries, polytechnics are poor cousins of universities, inadequately funded, poorly resourced and staffed and often teaching outdated technologies.

What sets the polytechnics in Singapore apart is that they have collectively formed the bedrock of Singapore's post-secondary landscape, accepting between them about 45% of school leavers, giving them a strong foundation for work or further study. They are provided with all the facilities that would be found in the best university colleges — including a complete range of sports facilities as well as performing arts centres, all supporting a wide range of out-of-classroom student activities. They also offer not only the basic diploma, but also further education in terms of advanced and specialist diplomas, and professional programmes. The Polytechnics run a wide range of classes after hours for working adults and are fully anchored in the polity of business, industry and the community.

Each polytechnic hosts a range of centres of excellence and industry partner-ships to keep abreast of developments and indeed to drive trends. They are well-funded for applied research projects to keep the teaching staff well-tuned to developing technologies and business models.

The urge to convert them to universities was strongly resisted by the govern-ment which was cautious about creating a large graduate pool which would be under-employed and doing the same job as a polytechnic graduate, but feeling frustrated. Instead, it set about creating avenues for upgrading in a structured and planned manner which suited the economic growth of the country. This is explored in more detail in Chapter 8.

The Polytechnics in Singapore are today recognised as one of the central drivers of economic growth. They have all established global linkages with companies and higher education institutions. About half of all polytechnic students travel abroad during their study, for exchange programmes, language immersion, internships or community service projects under different service learning schemes. The number being attached to global companies is increasing each year, with the institutions aiming for one local and one overseas internship or industrial attachment for every student.

The graduates are confident, familiar with work requirements and can contribute to a company productively without extensive retraining. Hence they are sought after by employers as shown by the annual employment surveys. It took 50 years from 1954 when the first polytechnic was established, but the polytechnics in Singapore have come of age, yet have retained their youth and vibrancy by constantly reinventing themselves.

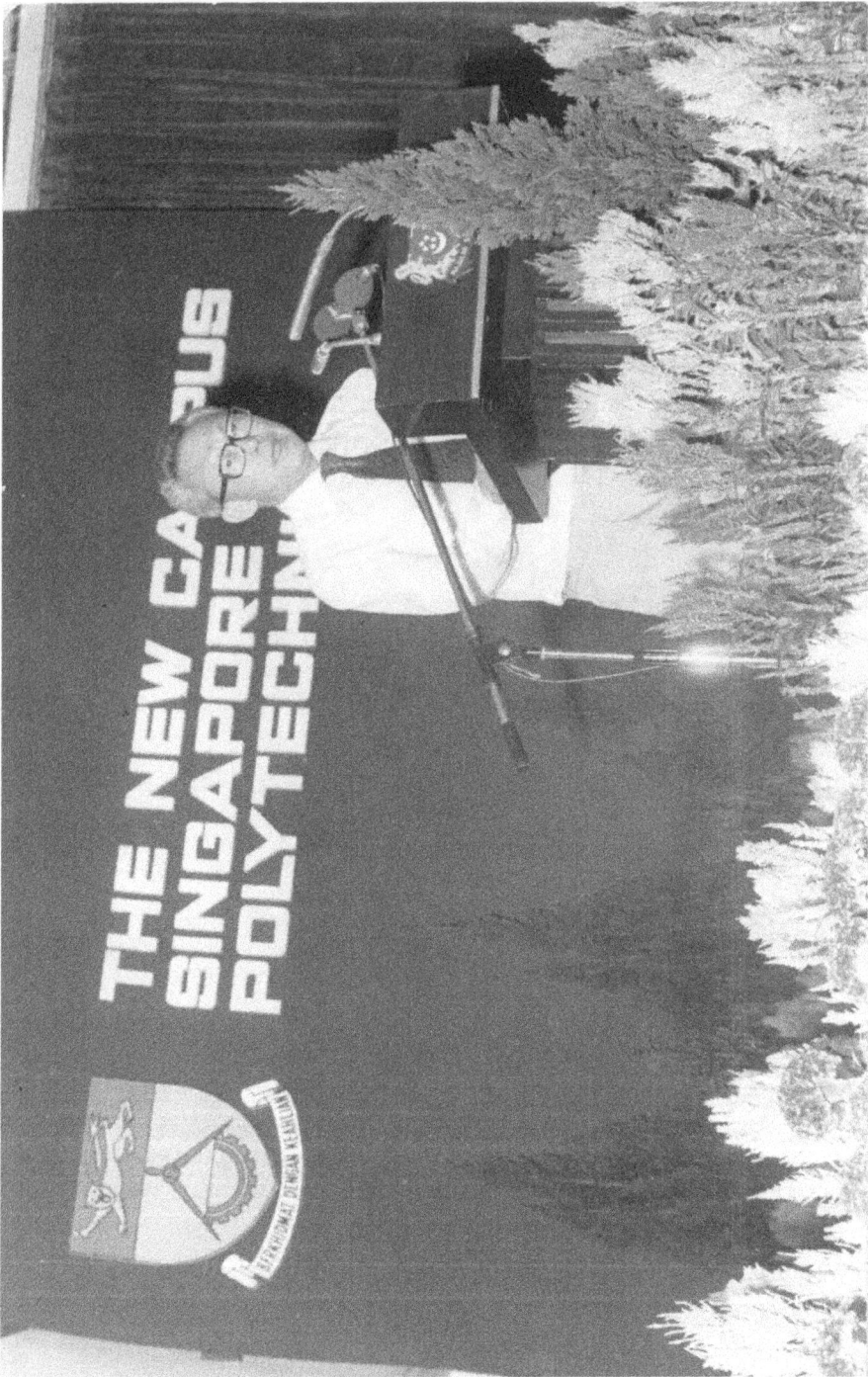

Former PM Lee addressing the invited guests when he officiated the opening of SP's Dover Campus in 1979.

First local SP Principal Mr Khoo Kay Chai (1976 to 1995) showing Former PM Lee a model of the Dover campus. Looking on were then Ministers Mr Ong Teng Cheong, Dr Ahmad Mattar (far left) and Mrs Lee Kuan Yew (far right) (official opening SP Dover Campus, 1979).

No. 4 of 1982

Ngee Ann Technical College (Amendment) Act 1982

1. This Act may be cited as the Ngee Ann Technical *Short title.* College (Amendment) Act, 1982.

2. The Ngee Ann Technical College Act is amended — *Miscellaneous amendments.*

(*a*) by deleting the words "Ngee Ann Technical College" in the long title and in sections 1, 2, 3, 17B and 17C and substituting in each case the words "Ngee Ann Polytechnic"; and

(*b*) by deleting the word "College" in sections 2 to 6, 8, 9, 11 to 14, 15A, 16, 17, 17A and 18 and in the Schedule and substituting in each case the word "Polytechnic".

Construction of contracts, gifts, etc. **5.** On and after the commencement of this Act, any reference to the Ngee Ann Technical College contained in any contract, agreement, bequest, will, trust or other instrument shall have effect as if it were a reference to the Ngee Ann Polytechnic.

CHAPTER 207   1985 Ed.

Ngee Ann Polytechnic Act

Ngee Ann College was renamed Ngee Ann Technical College in 1968. It was renamed Ngee Ann Polytechnic with the gazetting of the Act on 16 Apr 1982.

Continuing upgrading of equipment and technology to keep pace with industry competencies (2000).

A bird's eye view of Nanyang Polytechnic's Ang Mo Kio campus.

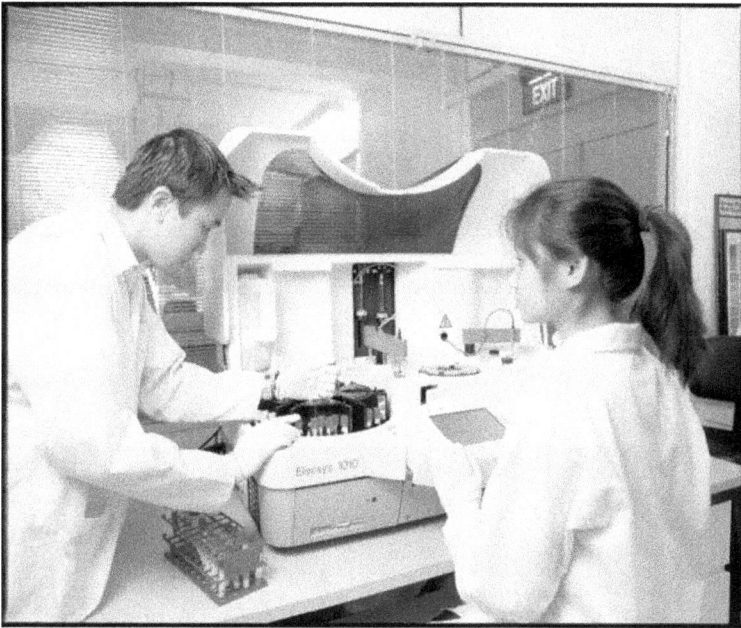

High Vacuum Magnetron Sputtering System for Chemical Sensor Fabrication, SP, 2001.

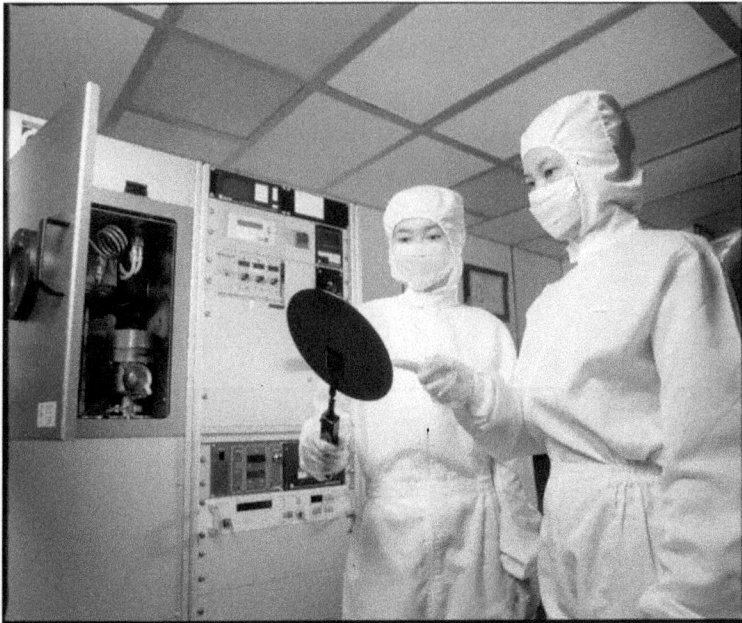

High-Tech Microelectronics Laboratory with a High Vacuum Sputtering System for Fabrication Works in the School of Chemical and Life Sciences, SP, 2001.

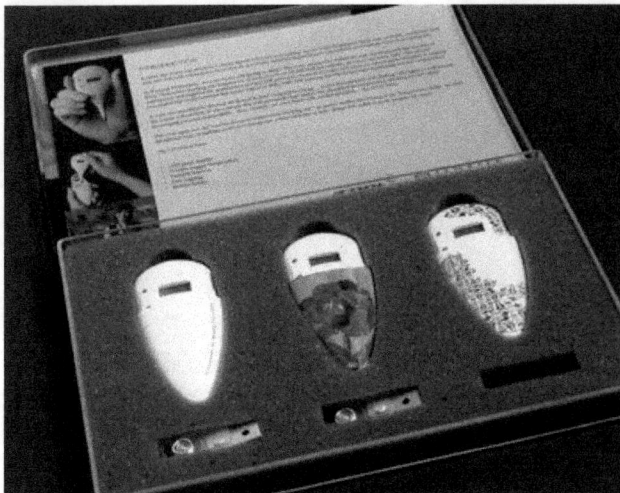

In April 2003, the Temperature Badge was developed by Temasek Polytechnic at the peak of the Severe Acute Respiratory Syndrome (SARS) outbreak.

NP's campus rejuvenation plan continues to keep the teaching and learning facilities, and sports and recreational facilities current and up-to-date.

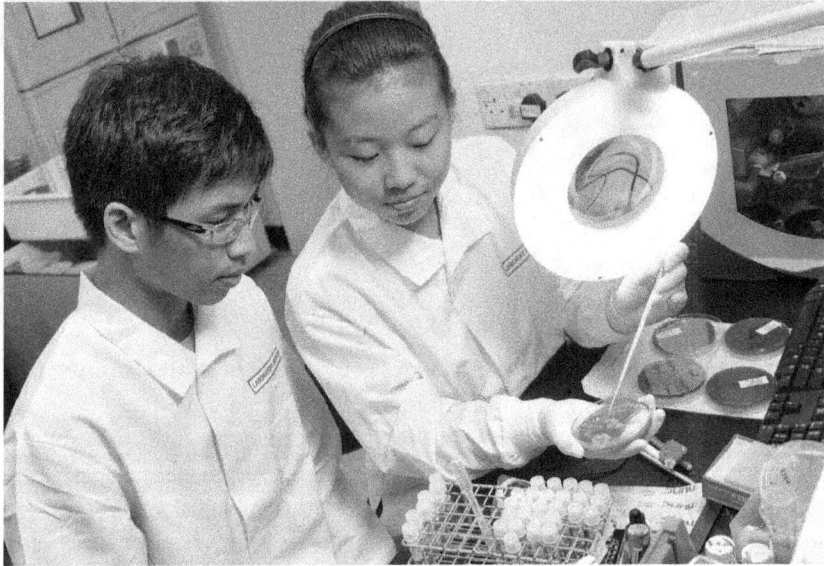

Hands-on training to offer innovative and practical solutions to some of the pressing challenges faced by local companies.

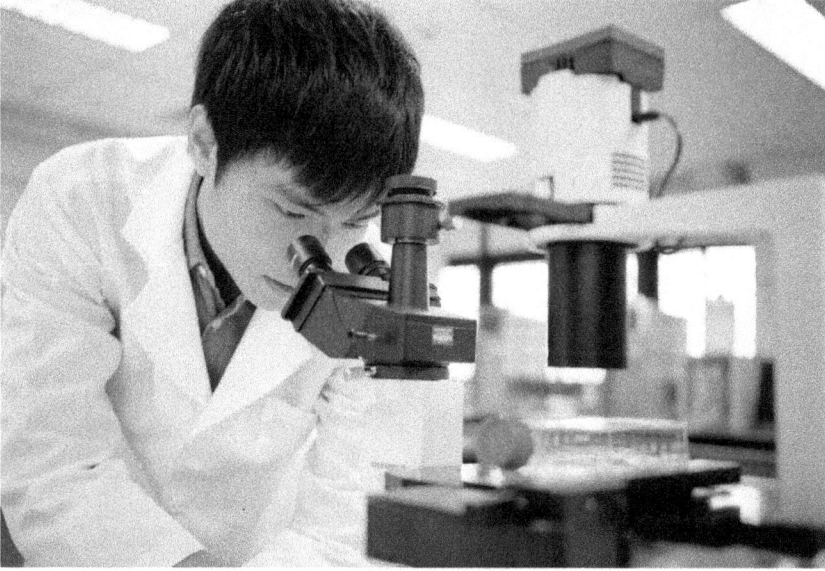

New centres to challenge and stretch students in practical solution-finding for industry.

Under the MOE Poly-Foreign Specialised Institute scheme, NP signs an MOU with Boston's Wheelock College, 2007.

Republic Polytechnic's Arts Centre at night.

A student dance performance at Republic Polytechnic.

Singapore Polytechnic's grand Administration Building.

One of the historic buildings from the British army base, converted to a students' centre at SP.

An example of Polytechnic Sports facilities, Republic Polytechnic.

Temasek Polytechnic Campus, designed by James Stirling and Michael Wilford.

Temasek Polytechnic is the only polytechnic that is certified as an Approved Maintenance Training Organisation by the Civil Aviation Authority of Singapore.

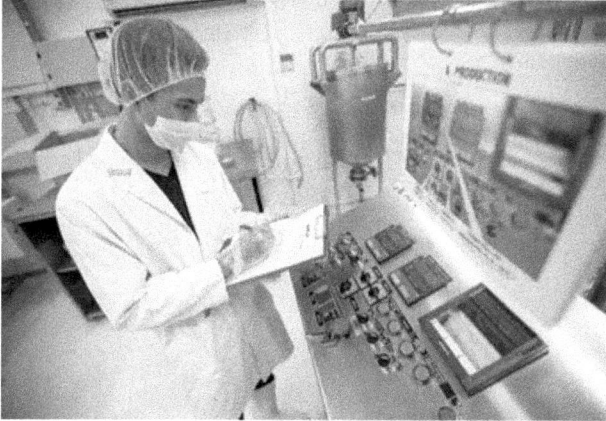

Temasek Polytechnic students using an ice-cream making facility learn about the various aspects of the food manufacturing business, such as product development, packaging design and process optimization.

CHAPTER 6

The Transformation of TVET

Landmark Events:

1991: Report of the Review Committee in Improving Primary Education
1992: Establishment of Institute of Technical Education to replace VITB
1994: Report of the CET Review Committee
1995: ITE 2000 Strategic Plan
1998: Rebranding VTE and ITE
2000: ITE Breakthrough Strategic Plan
2005: ITE Advantage Strategic Plan
2005: One System, Three Colleges Governance Model launched
2005: ITE College East opened
2010: ITE Innovate Strategic Plan
2010: ITE College West opened
2014: ITE College Central and HQ opened
2015: ITE Trailblazer Strategic Plan

As we saw in Chapter 3, the VITB has been the backbone of Singapore's vocational and skills training system since 1979. It had an excellent record of producing highly capable and well-trained manpower to fill the demand from business and industry. However, as the economy started to mature, demand for knowledge as a key aspect of a person's toolkit on the job began to appear.

Employers were not satisfied with primary school leavers, such as the Primary 8M and 8E leavers, topped up with a VITB skill certificate up to NTC-3. They wanted workers who had the full 10 years of schooling followed by post-secondary vocational training.

There was also significant wastage during the training. Sixty per cent of the trainees coming from the primary schools could not successfully complete their training, because their basic academic preparation in Mathematics and English was not adequate. Therefore the challenge confronting the Singapore education system was two-fold:

(a) To redesign the school system so that everyone would be able to complete at least 10 years of basic education, and
(b) To reposition vocational education as a post-secondary system.

These were two very significant challenges which, once successfully implemented, changed the face of TVET and can be considered a modern miracle of transformation. This chapter is devoted to how this was achieved.

The Impetus for Change

The turning point for VITB came in 1992 when the government decided on a significant economic restructuring process. This was a result of the charting of the next phase of Singapore's development, which meant a parallel restructuring of the school system.

By 1990, Singapore had emerged as a Newly Industrialised Economy, one of the Asian tigers together with South Korea, Taiwan and Hong Kong. The economy had been through several years of double-digit growth and had matured somewhat. Other regional economies were doing well, which meant numerous growth opportunities for Singapore companies.

The Strategic Economic Plan (SEP), an economic blueprint for Singapore's progress in the next 30 years, was unveiled in 1991. It set strategies and programmes for Singapore's next phase of economic restructuring and development, with a vision to make it a first league developed country. The way forward focussed on making the nation a centre of high-tech manufacturing industries and an international business hub, with local companies advised to concentrate on export and regional investment. This meant that the workforce needed to be brought up to speed.

Meanwhile, the then Minister for Education and current President of Singapore, Dr Tony Tan, set up a Review Committee in July 1990 to look into the school system, including vocational training. Policymakers had already recognised that the VTE system would no longer be effective in supporting the next phase of Singapore's rapid development. While the bulk of the secondary school cohort who joined the VITB were generally doing well, the same could not be said of those who entered after completing eight years of primary education.

While 85% of the latter group of students went into VITB, only 40% were able to complete the lowest, semi-skilled National Trade Certificate or NTC-3 course, largely due to the lack of competency in English and Mathematics. There were also many trainees who perceived the course as having low market value and dropped out, lured by better-paying factory or service sector jobs. The VITB's Graduate Employment Surveys conducted in the late 1980s had also revealed that 75% of this group, upon graduation, were not getting the jobs that matched what they had trained for. In addition, employers preferred vocational graduates with at least a secondary level education in view of the need for retraining to keep up with technological advances and economic changes.

Led by John Yip, who was then Director of Education, the 12-member Review Committee (which included the author) looked into curriculum needs, demands and expectations of the school system, issues with streaming, and vocational education and training. It also studied school systems in Germany and Japan to consider what could be utilised or modified to suit Singapore.

This report, released in March 1991 and titled "Improving Primary School Education" but more commonly referred to as the Green Book, changed the provisions in the Goh Report significantly. Streaming at the primary level was delayed by a year to Primary 4 when pupils were placed into classes of English, Mathematics, Science and mother tongue of varying difficulty, labelled as EM1, EM2 and EM3, all of which led to the Primary School Leaving Examination (PSLE). This, which used to be a pass/fail examination, was repositioned as placement exam. At the secondary level, the Normal course was subdivided into Normal (Academic) and Normal (Technical), and the latter had new technical subjects in its curriculum, the intention being to better prepare school-leavers for ITB/VITB training.

More importantly for technical education, there were two recommendations in the report that had a significant impact on how VITB would be restructured.

Firstly, the committee recommended that all pupils go through at least 10 years of general schooling, including at the secondary level, before advancing to the next level of education or training. Secondly, the committee proposed the establishment of a new secondary level technically-oriented course, named the Normal (Technical) course, which would strengthen pupils' proficiency in English and Mathematics while paving the way for vocational education and training.

This was a major shift in education policy which had previously required the academically weakest students to complete eight years of schooling before embarking on vocational training. It would allow pupils to have more options in that they could take either an academic route or a technical/vocational one to further their education and training, depending on individual interests, aptitude and potential.

As a consequence, the VITB would need to be restructured and reorganised as a post-secondary, tertiary institution providing vocational and technical education. It would also be necessary to build up its image as an option that could lead to further education and dispel fears that the VITB route was for failures. Such a change was going to be phenomenal and would require much thought and planning.

One of the key people involved at the onset of this metamorphosis of VITB was Dr Law Song Seng who was then helming the institute as its Director. Chairing an internal VITB Review Committee on "Upgrading Vocational Training", Dr Law led his team in proposing wide-ranging changes that encompassed restructuring of courses, apprenticeship schemes, better opportunities for trainees to achieve higher-level skills and progress to further their education and training as well as improvements in the training environment, and significantly, a name change.

In his book, "A Breakthrough in Vocational and Technical Education — The Singapore Story", Dr Law recalls the name change as being "...*a strategic step to move away from the word 'vocational' because of the deeply-rooted perception that "vocational training" and, hence, VITB, was the last place of resort for those who had failed in schools.*" Hence, to change societal mindset and attitudes towards vocational training, the deliberate decision to remove the term "vocational" from the institution's name and replace it with "technical" was made. This would better reflect the higher level skills courses provided by a post-secondary institution.

Thus was born the Institute of Technical Education, in April 1992, amidst much hope and excitement. Its establishment has been one of the most significant developments in the history of vocational training in Singapore. However, it would take more than two decades, with much strategic planning, hard work and perseverance, before this was fully appreciated.

The Role and Functions of the New ITE

For a start, the metamorphosis of the VITB to ITE required a clear articulation of how the latter would differ from its predecessors, the role it would play in shaping the future of vocational training and education in Singapore, as well as its contribution towards building the nation.

This was clearly spelt out during the inauguration of the ITE on 31 March 1992, by the late Dr Tay Eng Soon, Senior Minister of State for Education and Chairman of ITE. Dr Tay has been accurately described as "the prime architect" involved in changing the vocational training and education landscape in Singapore. A passionate advocate for the ITE who recognised the importance of skills to improving Singaporeans' lives, Dr Tay highlighted the mission and functions of ITE as follows[1]:

> *ITE's mission will be "to maximise the potential of Singaporeans through excellence in technical education and training in order to develop the quality of our workforce and enhance Singapore's global competitiveness". This mission statement reflects ITE's role and commitment in meeting the skilled manpower needs of our economy. To fulfil this mission, ITE will focus on the following five functions:*
>
> 1. *Provision, Promotion and Regulation of Technical Training and Education Courses*
> *As our economy moves upwards, ITE will expand higher-level technical training courses for secondary school leavers. New courses will be developed to meet industry's needs. School leavers will have a wider range of full-time and apprenticeship courses to match their interests and aptitude. ITE trainees will receive a well-rounded education, so that they are not only highly skilled, but also physically fit and socially responsible.*
>
> 2. *Upgrading Technical Skills of the Workforce through Continuing Education and Training*
> *However, there is still a large pool of untrained workers who do not participate in the existing CET programmes owing to various reasons. The ITE will be focusing on three new initiatives to help this pool of workers to come forward for training.*
>
> *i. TIME Programme*
> *It is designed for some 120,000 workers aged 40 and above to upgrade their skills and remain technically relevant in the next 10 to 20 years of their working lives. ITE has estimated that a realistic target for this group is 40,000. This programme, launched in December 1991, is conducted in 4 languages and has no formal entry requirements normally stipulated for young workers. This is to enable the majority of the mature workers who have little formal education a second chance for training.*
>
> *ii. A New Scheme to Train Adult Workers*
> *The second initiative is aimed at drawing unskilled young adult workers into part-time training programmes. ITE will be developing a new strategy to extend the existing MOST (part-time Modular Skills Training) Scheme to reach out to more workers in this category. ITE will be considering a new cooperative training approach in which employers will provide on-the-job training [that] complement day-release training at ITE institutes, an adult version of apprenticeship training.*

---

[1] Speech by Dr Tay Eng Soon, Senior Minister for Education at the inauguration of ITE, 31 March 1992, "Reliving ITE's Transformation", page 14.

iii. Formation of Advisory Council on CET

The third initiative that ITE will look into is the formation of an Advisory Council for the various CET programmes for workers. The Council, comprising representatives from employers, unions and government, can provide a more integrated approach in overseeing the implementation and promotion of all CET programmes, that is, BEST, WISE, MOST, TIME and the proposed training scheme for young adult workers.

3. *Regulation and Promotion of Industry-Based Training and Education in Technical Skills*
    The third major function of ITE is to further promote industry-based training. The ITE has two plans:

i. Expand the Scope of Apprenticeship

First, ITE will work closely with the industry to strengthen and expand the scope of apprenticeship in Singapore. I am happy to note that members of the Singapore Manufacturers' Association (SMA), which went on a mission to Germany and Switzerland last September to study the Dual System of Apprenticeship, are convinced of the merits of apprenticeship. The SMA has proposed that an Apprenticeship Council with employers, government and union representatives be set up to promote apprenticeship among employers and school leavers. This Council will focus on how to help SMEs meet their skilled manpower requirements through apprenticeship.

ii. Encourage Companies to Set up In-house Training Centres

The second plan is to encourage and help more companies to set up their own training centres. We now have about 48 company training centres accorded Approved Training Centre status. These centres have qualified industry trainers and training equipment to run courses leading to ITE certification. They also have the flexibility to tailor programmes to their specific needs and help train more people for the industry.

4. *Regulation of Certification and Standard of Technical Skills*
    As its fourth function, ITE will extend certification to emerging skills. As our economy becomes more service-oriented, ITE will extend the certification of service skills to other new areas besides Retail Sales, Health Care and Travel Services which are now certifiable. We will also identify more areas for certification at the highest National Technical Certificate Grade One or NTC-1 level.

5. *Promotion and Provision of Consultancy Services for Training and Education in Technical Services*
    The fifth function of ITE is to provide services to employers in training their workers. The ITE will help companies to identify training needs, develop training programmes, design instruction and train trainers. ITE will also support Singapore's role in the international community by sharing its experience and expertise in technical training.

During this same speech, Dr Tay also announced that seven new ITE institutes would be built and three existing ones upgraded over the next five to six years to the estimated tune of $250 million.

The significance of the inauguration address by the Minister was not lost on the staff of ITE nor industry. With the elevation of technical education to post-secondary level, the bar had been raised for technical education, to be aligned with the shift to high-tech manufacturing and services envisaged in the Strategic Economic Plan. Not only would the quality of students improve with 10 years of education, so would the scale. This new positioning of the ITE was the stimulus for the upgrading of all the ITE institutes.

The Remodelling of the ITE

Despite the clearly spelt out role of the ITE and the money pumped into its vast overhaul, its negative image persisted and much effort and dedication were needed to bring about a change in public perception and attitudes. Dr Law recalls in a column entitled 'Letters To A Young Public Officer: A Mission Made Possible', "The task was daunting, the key challenge being the rebranding of the VITB and changing the societal mindset and attitudes towards vocational training. The VITB had long suffered from a poor image, shunned by society as a last resort for failures in schools."

In addition to the image issue, there was a need for a clear vision for the Year 2000. A catalyst who got the ball rolling in the right direction was the Chairman of the ITE Board of Governors who took the helm in 1994, Mr Eric Gwee Teck Hai.

Although it was Dr Tay who championed the setting up of the ITE in 1992 as an important pillar of post-secondary education and served as Chairman of the VITB and ITE from 1981 to 1993, it was unfortunate that he never saw ITE become an institution that he would likely have been immensely proud of. After his untimely demise at the age of 53 in August 1993, Mr Gwee took over the reins as ITE Chairman in 1994. A Director at Esso Singapore Pte Ltd, he came with a private sector perspective.

Four key issues were identified as being critical:

— the need to build up an identity as a credible post-secondary institution,
— upgrading the professional capabilities of staff,
— physical development of the various institutes, and
— creating a "total learning" environment.

The negative image and status of ITE training relegated it to being the least favoured educational pathway, an option for students who failed. There was a need to enhance the quality of staff and groom Training Managers and Heads of Departments.

Mr Gwee agreed that there were many challenges, the key being an image change. The decision was made to focus on this area. In his own words, "Changing the image of ITE was nothing about glamour or fancy advertising. It was simply about how every graduate would be looked upon by others — opinion leaders and the public at large. To do that, we needed to understand the profile and traits of the students who came into ITE. The Board's priority was to work with the Ministry and engage the ITE management fully in building up a viable education system that will be readily accepted by students, parents, teachers and society as a whole."

It took three successive phases of development, each led by a five-year strategic blueprint, starting in 1995, to establish the ITE as a global leader in technical education. A fourth phase, which took place from 2010 to 2014, clinched its global recognition as an innovator in technical education. In 2015, ITE launched its fifth roadmap — ITE Trailblazer — to be a trailblazer in career and technical education.

The 4Ps Approach to Transformation

Underpinning these phases of remaking was the use of an integrated 4Ps approach, where each "P" represented an essential element for transformation as follows:

— People Transformation (Staff, Culture and Capabilities)
— Product Transformation (Certifications and Programmes)
— Place Transformation (Infrastructure and Learning Environment)
— Promotion Transformation (Image, Branding and Communications)

Phase One: ITE 2000 (1995–1999)

The first five-year Strategic Plan was entitled ITE 2000, with a vision to build the ITE into an established post-secondary technical institution by the year 2000. ITE's Deputy Chief Executive Officer (Corporate), Ms Sabrina Loi, recalls it as the toughest of the four Strategic Plans, as the process of creating such a roadmap was new to the staff and they had no reference point.

ITE 2000 recognised that ITE's training needed to cater to two key groups, namely, school leavers and workers. Therefore training programmes that would meet the ever-changing needs of the industry had to be designed for school leavers, especially those from the GCE Normal (Technical) Course, as well as students who had left school before completing 10 years of education. Training programmes would also be required to help people already working to upgrade and keep up to date with workplace changes.

ITE 2000 also aimed to create a network of 10 modern institutes in strategic locations near key population centres. Redesigning, rebuilding and upgrading ITE's physical facilities to meet the needs and expectations of school leavers would serve to entice them to opt for an ITE education.

It was also felt that leadership, social skills, planning and other life skills should be integrated into the ITE training. Hence, a conducive campus environment that promoted student learning and self-development in a holistic way was included as another ITE 2000 goal.

The need for staff to become professionally qualified so as to meet the needs of post-secondary students was also reflected in ITE 2000. The target was to upgrade both their pedagogic and professional competencies and qualifications. In addition, it would be critical to imbue in them an intrinsic spirit of care and concern for their students, along with a training approach that was more interactive, questioning, probing and challenging as well as consultative rather than one which was instructor-centred.

Addressing the issue of ITE's poor image was going to be another major challenge and one that would require many years of concerted effort in tackling. A Public Perception Study was commissioned to assess societal-bias against ITE. As a result of this study, a Brand Equity Index was developed in 1997, based on a comprehensive analysis of perceptions from focus group interviews and questionnaires involving eight response groups — prospective students, opinion leaders comprising teachers, parents, employers and the general public and the ITE population of students, graduates and lecturers. This would form the benchmark for measuring success as well as the basis for developing a marketing and branding strategy.

ITE 2000 set a plan to focus on promotional efforts in two key ways. One strategy was to proactively target secondary school students with the positive image and values of technical and skills training. The other was to foster better recognition of technical training by changing public misperceptions, and close any information gaps. Thus began the process to reposition ITE through a corporate branding programme, direct engagement with stakeholders and a series of media campaigns.

The first media campaign, "Make Things Happen", was held from 1998 to 2000. The key message of this campaign was that the contributions of ITE graduates are vital to Singapore's economy and the everyday lives of its people. A wide range of media was engaged and rapport was also built with media representatives to provide them with timely and newsworthy stories.

Face-to-face engagement was enhanced via a Networking System. This was started with secondary schools to disseminate information and tackle misperceptions through informal contacts, talks, open houses and publicity material. The status of technical training was also promoted through skills competitions with ITE taking the lead in spearheading Singapore's participation in the WorldSkills Competition in 1995.

In his assessment of ITE 2000 in the ITE 2000/2001 Annual Report, Mr Gwee noted that the vision of the ITE 2000 Plan had been realised. ITE had been successfully transformed into an established post-secondary technical education institution. An excerpt from his message highlights the following achievements:

"...an Image Equity Study by AC Nielsen in 2000 has shown that the public perception of ITE training as a viable alternative path in post-secondary education has improved. ITE is now an attractive choice for many school leavers.

Reinforcing this change in attitude towards an ITE education is our intake performance in FY2000. In terms of overall capture rate of school leavers, we exceeded the national target for ITE. With intake rates of 76%, 80% and 48% from the respective GCE N(T), N(A) and O level pools of available school leavers, we successfully enrolled a quarter of the annual school cohort. As a result, enrolment reached a high of 17,965 in FY 2000, vis-a-vis an expected enrolment of 16,310.

Likewise, our Continuing Education and Training (CET) programmes also recorded a total of 216,683 CET training places offered by ITE and its industry training partners. This was 9% above the number of training places achieved in the previous FY."

One of the most visible changes during the implementation of the ITE 2000 Plan was the development of modern and well-designed campuses providing a comprehensive range of training facilities. A 10-year ITE Physical Development Plan resulted in 10 campuses located in the population centres of Ang Mo Kio, Balestier, Bedok, Bishan, Bukit Merah, Clementi, Dover, Jurong, Tampines and Pasir Panjang.

The then Senior Minister of State for Education, Mr Peter Chen, noted in his speech in April 2000, at the 4th ITE Institute Day Student Awards Presentation Ceremony:

"Besides enhancing physical facilities, a great deal of effort has been expended to create the kind of campus environment necessary to provide a holistic education. Various

enrichment programmes have been put in place to enable ITE students to maximise their talent and develop leadership skills, while undergoing technical training. These platforms include Student Councils, ECA Clubs and Sports. Further exposure is provided through the running of co-operative shops, participation in ITE Student Seminars and National Skills Competitions. ITE students also display their talents in arts and music through public performances. The various opportunities and encouragement given to ITE students aim to develop them as active citizens, contributing towards nation building."

ITE 2000 also resulted in staff development initiatives that aimed to level up individual skills and qualifications. These included formal upgrading programmes, re-training programmes and industry attachments. For example, a Study Award Scheme helped increase the number of graduate training staff who could assume key professional and leadership roles while a Master Training Programme conducted by ITE partner, Ministry of Education, Youth and Sports, Baden-Württemberg, Federal Republic of Germany, enabled outstanding ITE staff to become mentors to colleagues. As a result of these initiatives, staff confidence, image and social status were enhanced. For ITE's commitment to people development, it was conferred the People Developer Standard in December 2000.

In addition, ITE's concerted marketing efforts in raising its profile earned it a Plaque of Recognition at the Singapore Marketing Award 2000. It also received the Outstanding QC Organisation Award 2000, for the second time, from the Singapore Productivity and Standards Board, for the achievements and contributions that ITE had made to the national Productivity and Innovation Movement.

Phase Two: ITE Breakthrough (2000–2004)

The second five-year Strategic Plan, ITE Breakthrough, was formulated with a vision to make ITE a world-class institution. ITE's Deputy CEO (Corporate), Ms Sabrina Loi, describes ITE Breakthrough as a "major paradigm shift". "*That was the plan whereby we revisited fundamental assumptions about VTE, revamped our certification, curriculum and pedagogic models, reengineered our processes and aligned our systems and services to be worthy of world standards.*"

With Singapore rapidly transforming into a knowledge-based economy, it was important for ITE to be effective, relevant and responsive, and to be able to turn its students from being "knowledge vessels to knowledge applicators". Under the ITE Breakthrough plan, a review of the curriculum and learning model so that it could be realigned with the changing needs of the global economy was deemed to be necessary. The ITE training system would need to be made more relevant and responsive and ITE's Continuing Education and Training system would have to be enhanced to support national efforts in lifelong learning. There was also an urgency to increase organisational capacity via the development of a learning organisation. In addition, it was decided that efforts to further improve the image and profile of ITE in technical training would continue.

In accordance with the plan, a new curriculum model was developed, in which 80% of time was devoted to core modules that focused on building up technical competency, with a breakdown of 70% for practical training and 30% for theory. In addition, electives were introduced to cater to students who wanted to take on a subject of interest within or outside their main course of study. Most importantly, the new model saw 15% of curriculum time allocated to life skills, namely teamwork, communication, thinking and problem solving, sports and wellness, career development and planning, and customer service. This change would help to strengthen students' technical, methodological and social skills and prepare them for lifelong learning and success in the global marketplace.

In line with the focus on knowledge application, pedagogy in the ITE was transformed. An interactive, process-oriented model called PEPP (Plan, Explore, Practise and Perform) was developed. Under the PEPP model, teachers guided students as they planned the work to be done, explored the information required, practised as they learnt and finally, competently performed what they had mastered.

By the end of Phase Two, ITE courses were reconfigured into four broad clusters — Engineering, Electronics & Info-Communications Technology, Applied & Health Sciences, and Business & Services. New courses were introduced to meet industry demands for manpower. A new ITE Certification System, the National ITE Certificate or 'Nitec' System, emerged in July 2002, to allow for greater flexibility in responding to new emerging areas and to better project the value of an ITE education and the competencies of ITE graduates. An Entrepreneurial Development Framework was also introduced to cultivate the spirit of enterprise.

By January 2001, the 10 ITE campuses were re-organised into two networks — ITE East and ITE West — of five campuses each. The aim of creating two networks was to further foster multi-disciplinary and cross-level learning. The network format allowed students to take electives in different campuses, as well as combine talents from different fields in project work, thereby contributing to better interaction and instilling identity and confidence.

The Continuing Education Training (CET) was restructured to achieve greater integration and synergy with pre-employment training. A new major initiative, "ReNEW" (Reskilling for New Economy Workforce) was launched in July 2003 to provide fast-track intensive programmes, additional ITE certification and new Post-Nitec certification courses to further enhance training opportunities and employability of both ITE graduates and working adults. The CET operations were also integrated within the two ITE Networks so as to achieve quality, relevance and responsiveness. E-learning was also extended to CET.

Interactivity and collaboration between campuses and across fields were further strengthened via the pioneering of the eTutor system in 2002, the onset of an online learning community in ITE. Teachers could assess students' work online, track their progress and communicate more efficiently through emails, live chats and discussion boards.

To reflect their enhanced competencies and the emphasis on their role as facilitators, ITE teachers were re-designated as "Lecturers"; they were required to participate in industry projects and attachments to enable them to stay abreast with industry developments, all of which further underscored ITE's image and status as a tertiary institution. A review of the ITE Teaching Service, held in 2002, resulted in an increase in qualification requirements for teaching staff, a redesigned compensation structure and the creation of four new career tracks — Teaching, Leadership, Specialist and Technologist — to cater to aptitudes and interest.

Another system, the eStudent, stated to be the first of its kind in the region, was also pioneered during ITE Breakthrough. This system provided a web-based platform for students to self-manage various administrative services, such as enrolment, financial transactions and application for financial assistance, module selection and timetable planning.

To further its image and profile building impetus, a second branding campaign, "ITE — A Force Behind the Knowledge-Based Economy", was launched. This campaign focused on ITE's relevance to the key growth industries and raised its profile as an institution of choice for technical education. This was augmented with support from political leaders, the media and stakeholders. In particular, the then Education Minister, Mr Teo Chee Hean, hosted the largest group of 43 Members of the Singapore Parliament in visits to ITE campuses in 2002, which garnered much media publicity and positively raised ITE's profile in the eyes of policymakers and the public alike.

Prospective students were also enticed to be part of ITE via the "Experience ITE Programme", a two-day attachment programme that allowed them to have fun with hands-on learning, while exposing them to ITE's state-of-the-art facilities and learning environment. An ITE Discovery Programme was established for secondary school teachers and teacher trainees for them to experience and appreciate the relevance of ITE training and enable them to provide guidance to students who would be more likely to do well in technical education. Periodic updates for school leaders on the changes and developments in technical education, along with parent seminars and roadshows, also aimed to establish ITE as a viable choice especially for hands-on learners.

ITE Breakthrough helped ITE graduates enjoy greater employability, as well as receive high satisfaction scores from employers. As a testimony to its success, in 2005, ITE became the first educational institution to win the Singapore Quality Award, a significant business award, for its overall excellence. This signalled a turnaround in the public perception of ITE.

Phase Three: ITE Advantage (2005–2009)

The vision for the third strategic blueprint, aptly named "ITE Advantage", was for ITE to become a global leader in Technical Education. It was a bold vision which sought to take advantage of new opportunities in a global landscape that was rapidly changing and produce graduates who could be not only 'work-ready', but also 'world-ready', able to stand tall amongst their international counterparts.

The blueprint focussed on 4 goals. Firstly, students must be made ready for a global environment that was getting more and more competitive. This would require ITE education to strengthen the integration of theory with practice through coursework, industry exposure and projects, nurture leadership and entrepreneurship skills, and inculcate a global skills-set and mindset in students and staff.

Next, lifelong employability must also be ensured for ITE graduates and adult learners, which meant greater flexibility in programme design and more immediately accessible short courses to provide relevant skills, along with joint certification schemes with industry partners.

The third goal was to expand ITE's global presence. This would be done via strategic alliances and collaborative partnerships with global players. The goal was not only to maximise learning opportunities for staff and students but also take ITE's programmes and services to other countries, for instance via international certification and consultancy, thereby strengthening ITE's global presence as a game-changer in technical education.

The last goal under ITE Advantage was to enhance staff capabilities and competencies to better equip them to prepare students for a global economy and to pioneer and set new benchmarks in vocational and technical education to help students adopt a global skills-set and mindset. Opportunities would be provided for staff to develop into subject or technology experts and a competency-based performance management system would be implemented. ITE would also focus on developing niche areas under its Centres of Technology and industry collaboration and projects involving staff would be stepped up.

The ITE Advantage blueprint resulted in the start of some sensational outcomes.

For one, learning was made holistic via the "Hands-on, Minds-on, Hearts-on" Education Philosophy that encapsulated a unique ITE Brand of College Education. This is aptly described in the publication "Transforming Lives Through Innovations in Technical Education — The Singapore ITE Story":

> *"'Hands-on' training equips ITE students with the knowledge and skills-set required on the job. 'Minds-on' learning nurtures creative and independent thinking and the ability to adapt; while 'Hearts-on' learning develops "complete" ITE students, with sound values towards self, others and the community and passion for lifelong learning."*

A slew of new courses were introduced during this period, in response to dynamic and rapid changes in industry. These included ITE's first niche diploma course, the Technical Engineer Diploma in Machine Technology, as well as Nitec courses in Games Design & Development, Banking Services, Early Childhood Education, Paramedic & Emergency Care, Media & Broadcast Design and Architecture & Space Design, to name a few.

One System, Three Colleges Concept

An important landmark in ITE's transformation was the "One ITE System, Three Colleges" Governance and Education model in 2005. Under this concept, ITE's 10 small campuses were regrouped and consolidated into three regional Campuses and renamed ITE Colleges. Each College was empowered to develop its own niche areas of excellence to enhance the flexibility and innovativeness of ITE Education, while the ITE Headquarters oversaw the entire system, certification, policy issues, branding and HR, and ensured quality standards. This change facilitated better interdisciplinary learning, provided a more vibrant campus environment and helped consolidation of resources.

More than anything, the 'Three Colleges' system was a game-changer in the perception of ITE. Instead of small institutes serving a local population, ITE became a major league player with mega-campuses. These campuses would rival top colleges and universities overseas in their design and range of facilities. Anyone walking through any one of the campuses would not fail to be impressed by the facilities and their organization. The change not only impacted visitors, but staff and students alike in giving them pride of place and recognition.

The first campus, ITE College East, started operations in 2005; ITE College West and ITE College Central became operational in 2010 and 2013 respectively. These colleges would be equipped with a comprehensive range of facilities and amenities for total development, such as modern workshops, laboratories, smart IT classrooms, and sports and recreational centres.

Collaborations with significant industry players like ST Aerospace, Autodesk Asia, IBM, Hewlett-Packard, Volkswagen, ABB (Sweden), Microsoft, HP, Medical Education Technologies Inc (Florida), Toon Boom (Canada) and the University of London, to name a few, led to a variety of benefits.

A significant advantage was in the development of Joint Certifications, state-of-the-art Centres of Technology (CoTs) as well as authentic learning facilities. CoTs in the fields of Industrial Automation Technology, Business and Engineering IT, Engineering Education Technology, Automation and Robotics, Metrology and Healthcare were set up. The push for authentic learning would, in time to come, result in the Healthcare Simulation Training Centre, Hair Spa and Design Training Centre, Boncafe Barista Training Centre, Hotel@College West, Amber@West Training Restaurant, Aerospace Training Centre and ITE-HP Centre of Technology in Application Lifecycle Management. These provided practical hands-on training in settings that mimic actual work conditions so that transitions to jobs in the industry could be made seamless without requiring further training.

Another significant benefit was in the area of enhancing staff capability development for organisational excellence. The Total System Capability initiative, introduced in 2007, sought to enhance staff professional capabilities in current and new areas, and across domains and disciplines, through staff attachments and training, knowledge exchange, and the undertaking of industry and consultation projects. Three levels of Professional Capability were defined. At Level 1, 'Know', the focus was on the acquisition of professional knowledge and skills. At Level 2, 'Do', staff would be equipped to undertake projects or consultancy work while at Level 3, 'Lead', they would develop expertise and standing to take the lead in such work.

As a result, staff were involved in commendable projects such as the "Puppetry Robotic Glove System", "Green Energy Mobile Office and School", and iDe'Lite

(Interactive Diagnostic Evaluation for Learning @ ITE). The last, a Service Training Pedagogic Tool that integrated effective video-based technology with service training pedagogy, attracted great interest from industry players and was recognised as one of the 2009 Innovations of the Year by the USA's League for Innovation in the Community College.

In addition, ITE provided consultation for Government-to-Government projects such as the setting up of the Vietnam–Singapore Technical Training Centre for the Vietnam–Singapore Industrial Park, Regional Vocational Training Centre in Marka, Jordan, and a special vocational training arm within Batam Polytechnic, Indonesia. A key player in this role of extending the ITE brand internationally through the sharing of its expertise was ITE Education Services, a consultancy arm formed in 2003.

Last but not least, global partnerships enabled students to partake in ITE's Global Education Programme that gave them a broader international perspective through student exchange, learning journeys, industry attachments, community service, as well as cultural and sports programmes. ITE students were also challenged to strive for more and stretch themselves through participation in local and international technology, sports and cultural competitions. This saw them clinching a significant number of prizes, awards and accolades, further boosting morale and ITE's image.

To further strengthen its position in the global arena, ITE organised the International VTE Conferences to share VTE trends and best practices, in 2006 and again in 2009. The third branding campaign — "Thinking Hands Create Success" — was also launched during this phase. The campaign, bent on tackling biases against ITE and technical education that still persisted, positioned ITE students as thinking-doers and promising young talents. This was followed by the "We Make You Shine" campaign that highlighted the outcomes and successes of an ITE education in order to encourage people to choose it as an alternative pathway to success.

ITE Advantage saw accolade after accolade being received for ITE's achievements. Locally, in an interview with The Straits Times, then Minister for Education, Mr Tharman Shanmugaratnam, proclaimed ITE to be "the jewel in Singapore's education system".

A World Bank Study concluded that "ITE has achieved significant breakthrough by establishing itself as a post-secondary institution. It has effectively rebuilt and transformed its former 'vocational' institutes into top-line educational colleges. ITE has given skilled occupations a new social and economic importance, creating viable careers for its graduates." Its experience in doing so was shared at a World Bank Workshop on "Leaders in Education and Training for Sustained Growth in Africa", which further strengthened its global presence with regard to VTE.

The icing on the cake was winning, in September 2007, the *Global IBM Innovations Award in Transforming Government*, conferred by the Ash Centre for Democratic Governance and Innovation at Harvard University's John F. Kennedy School of Government, USA. The Award recognised ITE's transformation of VTE in Singapore as "the world's most transformative government programme", which had had "profound impact on citizens' lives" and called it a "model programme" with potential for global replication.

Phase 4: ITE Innovate (2010 — 2014)

The vision for ITE Innovate was for ITE to be recognised as a "Global Leader for Innovations in Technical Education". To become such a leader, ITE would need to lead in Vocational and Technical Education (VTE) developments, be innovative, set new benchmarks and distinguish itself from other organisations.

ITE Innovate recognised that with an increasingly borderless world along with the challenges and opportunities it presented and an evolving, technologically savvy youth audience, to stay ahead of the game, ITE would have to "redefine and reinvent its educational approach, teaching and learning environment and modes of student engagement". This would include revamping its CET to go beyond satisfying industry demands and enhancing learners' employability.

Next, ITE Innovate would focus on strengthening and widening industry and global partnerships. Such linkages would foster innovations, ensure that ITE's programmes were industry-relevant, and further ITE's quest to expose students to authentic learning environments and real-life industry projects and applications.

Finally, ITE Innovate would enhance its capability for innovative excellence. Strategies to achieve this would include improving key systems, processes and services for enhanced organisational capacity, as well as developing staff to maximise their potential.

By the end of this phase, ITE offered a total of 101 courses (or programmes), a big leap in numbers from its humble beginnings. Besides continuing to bring in new courses to keep up with industry and workforce demands, ITE introduced a new Career Cluster Framework (CCF) in January 2014. Instead of preparing students for a single occupation, which in a rapidly evolving economy might quickly become obsolete, the CCF provides training for a cluster of related occupations, which would allow graduates to take on alternate specialisations and careers within the same industry. It was, again, a fundamental shift in the way ITE equipped its students to face the world of work.

To help Normal (Technical) students with less than two GCE 'N'-Level passes to cope with ITE studies, a three-year Enhanced *Nitec* Foundation Programme (e-NFP) was piloted in January 2014. In this programme, the curriculum was broken down into smaller, more manageable modules, supplemented by an academic foundation programme, to build the literacy and numeracy skills of these students.

For adult learners, an enhanced, more flexible CET Skills Qualification Framework was introduced in January 2012. It offered more streamlined programmes and shorter course duration that allowed participants to obtain qualifications in as short as 1.5 years, instead of three years. In line with Singapore's push to be a learning nation, a new approach to offer exciting opportunities for personal development and enrichment to a wider range of professionals and executives was adopted, and industry-based learning extended.

By the end of 2014, ITE had inked over 100 Memoranda of Understanding (MOUs) with industry and global partners, such as Rolls-Royce, Marina Bay Sands, Australia's Holmesglen Institute, L'Oreal, Resorts World Sentosa, Eurocopter, Adobe, Yokogawa Engineering, Bosch Rexroth, Huawei International, McDonald's Restaurants, Korea Polytechnics, Denmark's Tech College Aalborg, and Germany's Kaufmännische Schule Göppingen, to name a few. These MOUs enhanced ITE's global standing and presence in VTE and provided many authentic learning and development opportunities for ITE staff and students. Under the Global Education Programme that leveraged on ITE's network of partners, an unprecedented 33% of the student cohort took part in overseas exchange initiatives, industry attachments, community service, and/or cultural and sports activities.

During ITE Innovate, ITE hosted more than 1000 overseas visitors annually, the likes of which included presidents, royalty, ministers and high-ranking government officials, as well as representatives from prestigious organisations, from around the world to share its expertise in vocational and technical education.

It also collaborated with several countries such as Vietnam, Cambodia, the Philippines, and India to provide Train-the-Trainer programmes for specific occupations, training in pedagogy as well as other leadership and customized training programmes. These were for not only trainers but also administrators and institutional leaders. ITE's subsidiary, ITE Education Services Pte Ltd, also provided expertise towards developing a Model Skills Training Centre in Abuja, Nigeria and a World-Class Skills Development Centre in India.

Total System Capability to enhance staff's professional capabilities continued during this phase. 92% of staff achieved the "Do" or "Lead" levels of involvement in industry or consultancy projects in FY2013, a 54 percentage-point improvement from the time it was implemented, six years ago in 2007. In addition, in August 2010, the "REAL" Leadership Learning Series was started. The series aimed to build up ITE staff's leadership capabilities via learning from sharing and insights provided by industry chiefs and leaders. The ITE Academy, set up in 2013, further strengthened the training and development of ITE's core values and niche VTE competencies of its staff and training partners.

ITE Innovate was also profiled when the inaugural ITE Fiesta was held, in 2011. The aim of this Fiesta, which became an annual affair, was to showcase ITE's facilities, staff and student capabilities as well as highlight the opportunities available to secondary school students, parents and the general public. It also allowed ITE to engage with the community via a plethora of activities each year. These included free makeovers, haircuts, and health checks for senior citizens, free courses on air-con maintenance, computer repair, dance and cooking, and activities like LAN gaming and floral arrangement, to mention a few.

In May 2013, ITE launched ITE Epitome, its training and commercial facility located at ITE College Central. The first of its kind among Institutions of Higher Learning, the facility offered products and services — such as hair, fashion, floral and opticianry services, as well as pastries and coffee by ITE's own Delicatessen Café — from ITE's academic courses. Established brand names like Hoya Lens, and Jean Yip Group, lent their weight to this initiative by setting up shops within Epitome, to mentor and train students. As the facility is open to members of the public, students also obtained relevant work experience within the school, via interaction with real customers.

ITE students continued to shine in national and international competitions, winning medals at both local and worldwide events such as the ASEAN Skills Competition and the WorldSkills Competition. At the WorldSkills Competitions, the Singapore team, comprising students from the polytechnics and ITE, had its best showing when it was ranked 6th among 51 countries in 2011, while in 2013, it continued to do well, achieving 7th place.

ITE also received many accolades and awards for its efforts and commitment to organisational excellence and innovation. These included various HR and Best Employer Awards as well as the Public Service Premier Award for Organisational Excellence in the Public Sector, making ITE the first and only educational institution to receive this award. Yet another feather in its cap was becoming the first educational institution to be conferred the Singapore Quality Award with Special Commendation in 2011, a strong endorsement of ITE's systems and processes. ITE was also cited as an example of Singapore's education miracle by *The Economist* in March 2011, and recognised worldwide as a global leader in technical education in the OECD Publication titled *Strong Performers and Successful Reformers in Education: Lessons from PISA for the United States in 2010*.

It was also during ITE Innovate that the "I Believe" campaign was launched.

ITE Trailblazer (2015–2019)

In Feb 2015, ITE announced the launch of its latest blueprint, ITE Trailblazer, its strategic response to Singapore's next phase of development as an advanced economy and society. The basis for much of this blueprint was the recommendations from a committee that had been tasked to review the polytechnic and ITE education sector, along with career and academic progression prospects for the graduates there, as well as a Tripartite council responsible for developing and driving initiatives to ensure an integrated system of learning, pre- and post-employment, for all Singaporeans.

ITE Trailblazer was launched just after the debate and discussion arising from the ASPIRE Report and the establishment of the SkillsFuture Committee (see Chapter 9). This debate was on how education should evolve and the need for mindsets of people to change. Therefore, it is no surprise that it is aligned with SkillsFuture. The aim over the next five years was to chart new ground as ITE positions itself as "A Trailblazer in Career and Technical Education". The expected outcome is a move away from the existing trade-specific preparation model towards a more career-oriented, professional skills preparation model.

The two key elements of the blueprint are innovation to open up new pathways to help graduates become successful in their careers and life, even in an uncertain future, and a shift from a vocational, skills-for-a-trade focus to a skills-for-careers emphasis. This would mean equipping students with a strong and holistic foundation in technical skills, supplemented by workplace skills gained through internships to enhance skills competence and mastery.

Under this Plan, ITE will focus on the following four key strategic thrusts:

1. **A dynamic curriculum and an adaptive system**

   ITE will adapt and transform its learning environment and curriculum in tandem with industry changes and national economic directions, so that graduates are empowered to master specialised skills while being adaptable to industry changes. New paradigms in career-based technical education will be created. Students will have new pathways and upgrading opportunities, along with new industry 'place and train' (this has now been renamed as 'Earn and Learn') programmes for skills deepening and mastery, even after they have graduated. ITE learning will have strong foundations in core technical and 21st century competencies, strengthened by valuable life skills and work ethics.

2. **Making teaching engaging and learning empowering**

   In moving towards a culture of lifelong learning, new ways of teaching and learning will be introduced. This will involve greater incorporation of info-communication technology, reinvention of learning spaces and teaching methods that are tailored to different disciplines. Students will have more opportunities for authentic, flexible and self-directed learning, both in and out of ITE, to prepare them for contributing effectively to the global economy.

3. **Providing a holistic educational experience**

   ITE will provide rich and diverse learning experiences that will include diverse personal development and enrichment programmes, structured platforms to enhance career counselling and access to greater learning support. Through these, students can discover their talents and interests, realise their full potential, see new channels for success, visualise various career possibilities and engage in activities that benefit society. By developing well-rounded students, ITE's objective is for employers to appreciate the value of its education and be willing to pay a premium for its graduates' skills.

4. **Enhancing strategic collaborations and nurturing staff**

   New models of industry collaboration will be established. Progressive and committed employers and global partners, the community, and alumni will be roped in to take stronger ownership of developing students, beyond their classroom learning. The close, symbiotic relationship with industry and global institutions has been ITE's hallmark and will continue to ensure industry relevance and high employability for students. Through such relationships, staff will also be nurtured to grow their passion and develop skills mastery.

The first four strategic plans, over a 20-year period from 1995 to 2014, can be said to be the foundational masterplan for transformation of TVET in Singapore, from lowly, last choice option to one that is well-accepted, well-branded and which provides opportunities for continuous upgrading and career progression. This will be even more pronounced and enhanced under the SkillsFuture initiative of 2014/15. TVET has come of age and has become a respected part of post-secondary education, industry collaboration and national consciousness.

Each plan stood on its own, but built on the previous one. No one could have anticipated the success at the beginning. But the crucial factors were certainly the visioning by government leaders, skilled execution by successive management, and deep support and involvement by business and industry.

How did ITE manage to carry all its staff, faculty as well as administrative and support staff through this transformation?

The Values behind the Transformation

Underscoring the four phases of transformation and beyond are ITE's mission, vision and values. Referred to as the ITE Heartbeat, these encapsulate its spirit and commitment to deliver the best value in education to meet the needs of students, industry and the community

Of particular mention are the ITE Values, aptly phrased as "ITE Care", which stands for:

- **Integrity** — being honest and sincere in words and actions towards others
- **Teamwork** — working and helping one another as a team to achieve
- **Excellence** — giving one's best in everything one does to add value to customers and stakeholders
- **Care** — caring for staff, customers and other stakeholders, the community and the environment

ITE Care was formulated as a result of feedback sought from staff as to what they felt were important values that would underpin the organisational culture of ITE.

The ITE Care culture permeates the organisation and is considered "a unifying force, touching the lives and hearts of students and staff". Staff have also observed that ITE Care has helped to attract caring and passionate people from the industry into ITE and to retain them. It has been described as a hallmark of ITE's brand of vocational and technical education.

In the words of Dr Law Song Seng, "… *the ITE Care" culture is what matters most. Students who come to us feel that they have failed, have low self-esteem and are unsure if they have a future. Teachers at ITE need to support and encourage them, and to understand their needs and help them. The success of ITE is measured not by what the management and staff have done, but by the success of the graduates."*

The Role of Image Building in the Reinvention of ITE

A critical success ingredient in the ITE reinvention recipe was changing its image in the eyes of the public. While this has been touched upon earlier, it is worthwhile looking a little more deeply into ITE's journey of rebranding and repositioning.

As had been mentioned, first VITB and then ITE were initially plagued by a deep-rooted societal preference for academically inclined students, information gaps about the institution and misconceptions about the value of its education and training. Therefore, it had an uphill task in gaining public recognition and raising its prestige. It took a bold, unprecedented rebranding strategy that spanned more than a decade to turn this image around and it involved an integrated system of communications, marketing and rebranding at strategic and tactical levels.

Strategic intervention involved creative branding campaigns, proactive media engagement and Public Relations initiatives, while tactical strategies included extensive direct engagement with key stakeholders to educate them and change their perceptions about ITE and its valuable contribution to Singapore's education landscape.

To begin with, ITE had to identify its key target audiences, get a better grasp on how it was perceived by them and how best to reach them. Hence, ITE embarked on an extensive mission to gather data via focus group discussions followed by a Public Perception Survey conducted by AC Nielsen (Singapore), an independent research company. From this initial research was born the first of ITE's public branding campaigns in 1998. Such a creative branding campaign was not something that other public educational institutions at that time had embarked upon. Subsequently, four more branding campaigns would be rolled out on a three-yearly basis, each aligned to the strategic blueprint for that period. These were all professionally commissioned and executed through advertising media such as newspapers, posters, buses and trains.

The maiden campaign "ITE makes things happen" took place from 1998–2000. The focus for the campaign was to create an appreciation for technical skills and their importance to everyday lives. Campaign visuals had a scientific, technological feel to them. The second campaign, "ITE — A force behind the knowledge-based economy" (2001–2003), had visuals showcasing key growth industries and ITE's relevance and contributions to them. This was followed by the "Thinking hands create success" campaign from 2004 — 2006. This campaign aimed to portray ITE students as uniquely talented "thinking doers"; visuals were of confident, talented youth aspiring towards success with the "Hands-on, Hearts-on, Minds-on" education from ITE.

The 2007–2009 Campaign, "We make you shine", positioned ITE as an alternative route to success. Visuals centred on ITE graduates' aspirations and desire to achieve inspirational goals with real-life examples of graduates who had become success stories in their fields. The message conveyed was that an ITE Education brought out the creative and innovative best in students, enabling them to be confident, passionate and able to hold their own in a global economy.

The fifth Campaign, "I believe" (2010–2012) aimed to enhance the profile of ITE students by focusing on their capabilities and values. The visuals shouted vibrancy and confidence, portraying ITE graduates who were positioned to take on the world as a result of their ITE education.

The latest Campaign, "Ready for the World" (2013–2015) reinforced that ITE graduates are armed with skills and talents, and ready to take the world by storm. The visuals showcase ITE students in their trade areas, full of passion, confidence and drive, ready to take on challenges the world throws at them.

The above campaigns were supported at a tactical level, and focussed on reaching out to students, teachers, parents, political leaders and the community. For example, engaging with political leaders, both locally and overseas, not only showcased to them the high quality of education students received but also garnered positive media coverage. There was much political endorsement from the likes of the Prime Minister, Deputy Prime Ministers and other key Ministers, which helped boost ITE's reputation especially on home ground.

Face-to-face initiatives included active networking with schools and teachers, and parent-targeted programmes. Part of the networking efforts was the establishment of a Career Services Centre, and an ITE Discovery Programme for secondary school teachers and trainee teachers. Parents were invited to attend seminars, held in English, Chinese and Malay, so that they could better understand the ITE brand of education and view the learning environments that their children would have access to.

Annual promotional talks for future potential students from secondary schools were another important component of the ITE publicity calendar. A two-day innovative camp called the "Experience ITE Programme" was put in place for

Secondary 2 and 3 students to allow them to get a feel of an ITE education and its role in the economy and society. This camp exposed them to a range of hands-on manufacturing, office and service skills required in the real world, through an integrated simulated learning system. There were also regular marketing activities such as open houses, road shows and more recently, the ITE Fiesta. Last but not least, participation of ITE students in local and international skills competitions like the WorldSkills Singapore and WorldSkills International, and then publicising their achievements at such events, helped to showcase students' talents and the value they brought to the table.

Through these various activities and by building good relations with media representatives, providing timely and newsworthy stories, effectively using the vernacular media, and being readily accessible to the media, ITE received publicity to the tune of 2,000 positive media mentions annually in recent years.

Public Perceptions Studies were conducted after the completion of each campaign so that ITE could measure perceptions shifts, as well as identify gaps and modifications needed for greater impact. Slowly but surely, ITE's image continued to grow positively. This was measured using a brand-equity tracking model, referred to as the Brand Equity Index (BEI), which covered 16 image attributes.

According to Dr Law, "the steep turnaround in the image of ITE was attributed to the convergence of three milestone events — through the opening of the first regional mega campus at ITE College East, the public endorsement of ITE's "Hands-on, Minds-on and Hearts-on" education by Prime Minister Lee Hsien Loong at the National Day in 2005, and ITE winning the Singapore Quality Award in 2005".

In FY2012, the Brand Equity Index was 70%, a whopping increase from the 34% baseline in 1997. This was a very impressive 106% improvement over a 15-year period. This improvement was evident across many target respondent groups. For example, the score for parents was 76% (from 20% in 1997) while for the general public it was 62% (from 23% in 1999). As a result, ITE could expect that employers would appreciate the value of its education and be willing to pay a premium for its graduates' skills. This is not something ITE would have been able to do even 10 years ago.

The transformation of ITE and with it, the whole TVET movement is going to be critical for all nations and economies going forward. As the world moves towards recognising and paying people for the knowledge-based skills they have instead of just theoretical understanding, skills-based education will be a premium in the future. This is now shaping new educational thinking in Singapore and other countries.

However, the chase for paper qualifications is ingrained in many newly-emerging countries in Asia as well as in developed countries. The transformation story in this chapter therefore holds multiple lessons for policy-makers and educational planners. The Singapore story of transforming TVET into a post-secondary option, and where students are valued by their lecturers and graduates by their employers, is definitely worth studying in detail.

ITE organised the first National Skills Competition in 1994.

ITE'S BRANDING CAMPAIGNS

FIRST BRANDING CAMPAIGN (1998–2000)

ITE — Make Things Happen

Phase 1

Phase 2

SECOND BRANDING CAMPAIGN (2001–2004)

ITE — A Force Behind the Knowledge-based Economy

Phase 1

Phase 2

Phase 3

THIRD BRANDING CAMPAIGN (2004–2007)

Thinking Hands Create Success

Phase 3

Phase 2

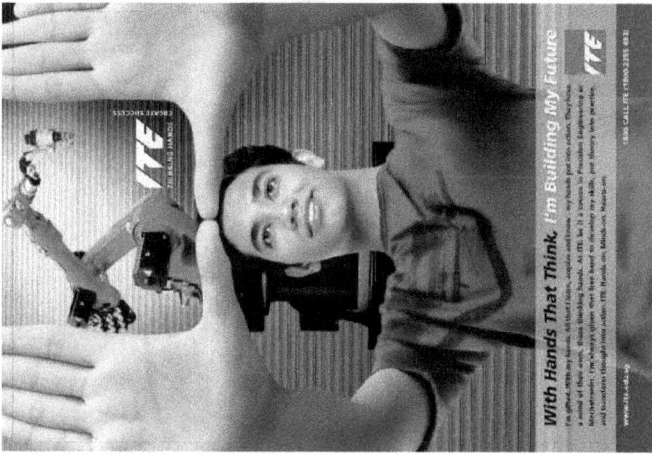

Phase 1

FOURTH BRANDING CAMPAIGN (2008–2009)

We Make You Shine

Phase 1

Mission: Triumph over challengers in the virtual world

Jerica Wee, ITE Graduate and Digital Animator

With my passion and self-belief, and ITE's unique College Education, my potential is nurtured to its fullest. I can animate my dreams to reality, and bring new dimensions to life in the digital realm. With these market-ready skills, I am poised to shine in the global economy.

We Make You Shine

www.ite.edu.sg

1800-CALL ITE (1800-2255 483)

Phase 2

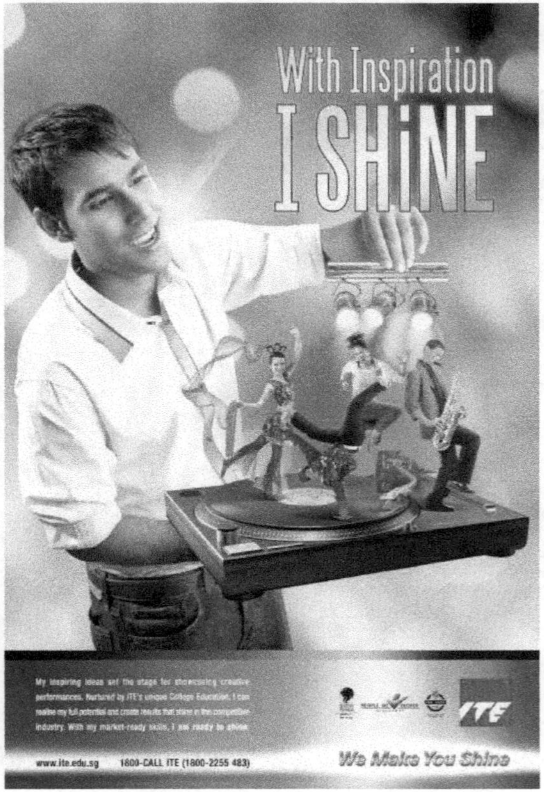

With Inspiration I SHINE

My learning ideas set the stage for showcasing creative performances. Nurtured by ITE's unique College Education, I can realise my full potential and create results that shine in the competitive industry. With my market-ready skills, I am ready to shine.

www.ite.edu.sg   1800-CALL ITE (1800-2255 483)

We Make You Shine

FIFTH BRANDING CAMPAIGN (2010 – 2012)

I Believe

Phase 1

Phase 2

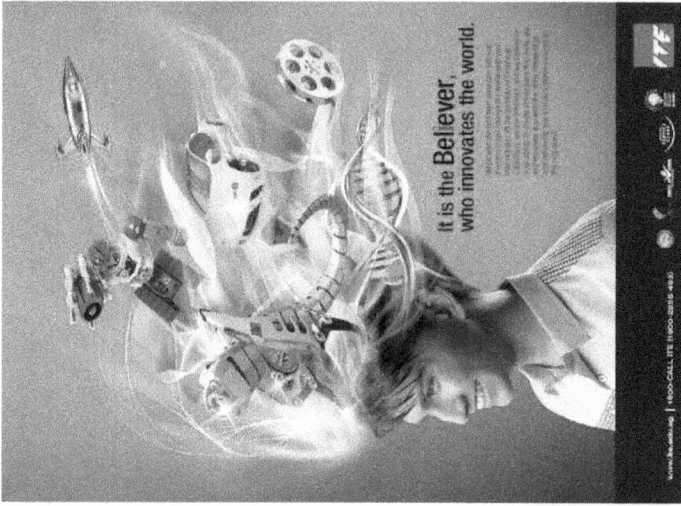

Phase 3

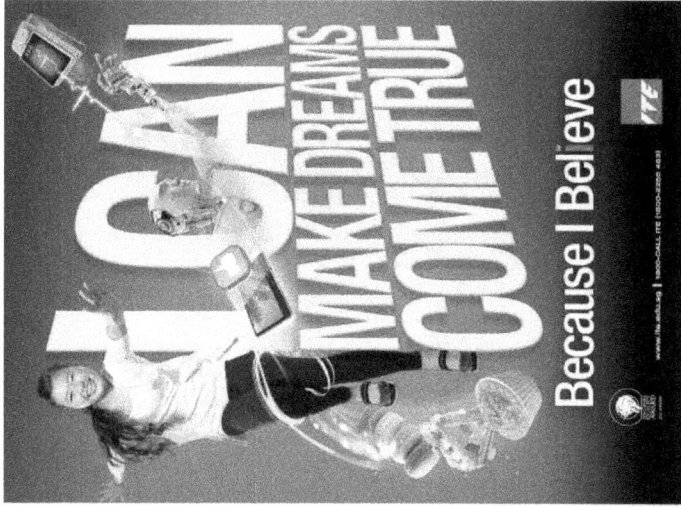

SIXTH BRANDING CAMPAIGN (2013–2015)

Ready for the World

Phase 1

Phase 2

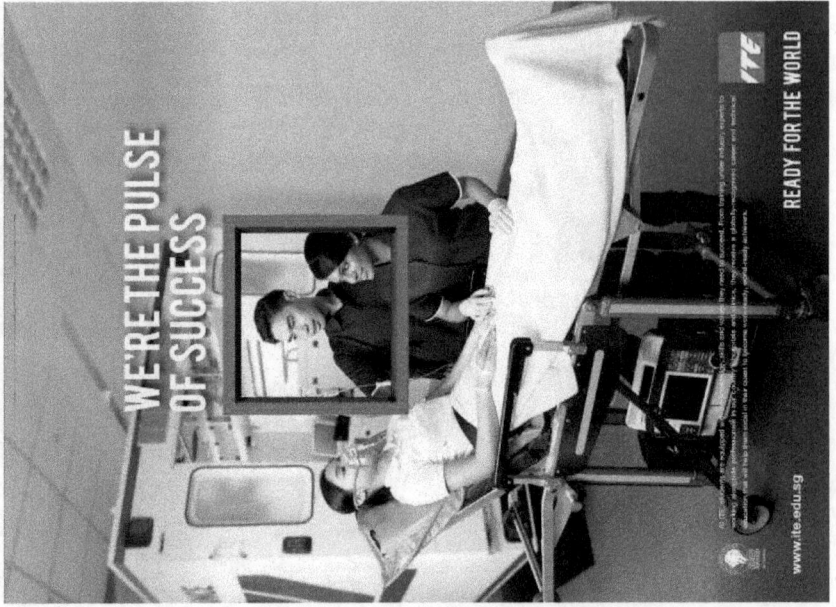

First Regional Campus ITE College East opened at Simei Avenue in 2006.

ITE College West, located at Choa Chu Kang Grove, opened in 2010.

ITE Headquarters opened in 2013.

ITE College Central opened in 2013.

ITE received the IBM-Innovations Award in Transforming Government from Ash Institute of Democratic Governance and Innovation in 2007.

ITE launched its second and third waves of transformation — ITE Breakthrough (2000 to 2004) and ITE Advantage (2005 to 2009).

ITE launched its fourth and fifth waves of transformation – ITE Innovate (2010 to 2014) and ITE Trailblazer (2011 to 2015 to 2019).

CHAPTER 7

The Labour Movement and Worker Upgrading

Landmark Events:

1982: Launch of BEST Programme

1987: Launch of WISE classes

1982: Establishment of NTUC Computer Training Centre

1997: Launch of Skills Redevelopment Programme (SRP)

1997/98: Asian Financial Crisis

2000: National Skills Recognition System established

2001: Lifelong Learning Fund created by Government

2003: Workforce Development Agency (WDA) established

2004: NTUC Learning HubPte Ltd established

2007: Vocational and Technical Training launched to upskill blue collar workers

2007: Start of Global Financial Crisis

2008: Employment and Employability Institute (e2i) launched

2008: Skills Programme for Upgrading and Resilence (SPUR) launched

2013: NTUC LearningHub trained more than 1 million workers

2015: NTUC LearningHub trained more than 1.7 million workers

In considering formal pre-employment education, one should not ignore the critical role played by the trade union movement in Singapore to promote worker upgrading through the provision of training from basic education to skills upgrading. This movement has been led primarily by the leadership of the National Trades Union Congress (NTUC) which has been able to create the economies of scale needed for large-scale upgrading as well as leverage its government connections for financial support even in the face of several economic downturns, particularly the global financial crisis of 2007–09.

From the early days of vocational and technical education, NTUC has been represented in the boards and advisory committees of the various training institutions of the government, namely the Polytechnics, the ITE and its predecessors. This has given the workers' representatives a bird's eye view of formal training systems, certification and qualifications. However, closer to their mission has been the need to ensure lifelong employability of its members and those of its affiliate unions.

Basic Adult Education

In the 1970s and 80s, the industrial workforce suffered from legacy issues of poor or no education during the colonial period and immediately after independence. They were found wanting in the necessary education and skills for the economic restructuring programme to be successful. A better-educated and skilled workforce was required to run and maintain automated and computerised machinery and systems in the restructured high-wage economy. However, in 1980, it was found that seven out of every ten workers had studied at most up to primary school level. About 17% of professional and technical workers had primary or no qualifications.

Basic literacy and numeric skills were needed so that workers could understand the language and operations of machines and equipment. To cater to the needs of workers who had missed out on basic education, the NTUC in collaboration with the Vocational Industrial Training Board (VITB) initiated the Basic Education for Skills Training (BEST) programme in 1983. This programme was designed to help workers who had not completed primary education to attain Primary Six level proficiency in English and Mathematics, the minimum requirement needed then for skills training at vocational institutes. Worker Improvement through Secondary Education (WISE) classes were started in 1987 to provide an avenue for those who had completed the BEST programme to improve themselves and obtain the GCE 'N' level qualifications.

The BEST and WISE classes were offered in companies, night schools and union education centres. Between 1983 and 2004, a total of 859,600 training places were taken up for the two programmes. Slightly more than a third of these places (310,883) were offered through the NTUC's training centres.

Computer Awareness and Skills Training

In 1982, NTUC started it first training centre, a simple computer training centre. This was to provide workers with basic training in computer applications such as word processing and spreadsheets. These skills were quickly becoming standard requirements in many job functions across business and industry, and workers needed to be brought up to speed quickly to keep their jobs or be replaced by a younger generation of better-equipped workers. Over the years, the NTUC has emerged as one of the biggest providers of basic computer courses. Between 1982 and 2004 over 300,000 training places were taken up through the NTUC computer training centres. Union members are given training grants and subsidized places at these centres.

Productivity Education for Unionists

The training of unionists in productivity concepts and practices took on a higher profile in the 1980s. These courses were designed primarily to give grassroots unionists and industrial relations officers a better understanding of the concept of productivity and its contributory elements. They imbided a productivity mindset amongst unionists whose support was necessary for successful implementation of programmes. Topics covered in courses for unionists include teamwork and teambuilding, work motivation, decision-making, the role of union leaders in productivity, problem-solving, worker participation, small group activities and labour-management relations. In later years, it included topics like ISO 9000 as well productivity measurement workshops for example on Economic Value Added (EVA). The latter was necessary as unionists needed to understand that productivity was no longer just about producing more with less but about total factor productivity and the value that labour adds to the production process. Factory visits to companies with good practices were also organized for unionists and books were published by the NTUC to showcase and share successful QCC and WITs ideas. Unions were also encouraged to include clauses in the Collective Agreements to contain some form of productivity commitment.

NTUC Learning Hub

In 2004, the computer training centre was corporatized as NTUC LearningHub Pte Ltd with the mission to enhance the lifelong employability of Singapore's workforce by providing high quality, innovative products and affordable learning. The training programmes provided by NTUC LearningHub include Infocomm Technology, Professional IT Certificates, Soft Skills & Literacy, Workplace Safety & Health, Employability Skills System, Customer Service Training, Trades, Cleaning, WSQ Security and Manufacturing Skills.

To date, it has trained more than 1,700,000 executives and working adults, and has worked with more than 10,000 companies to identify training needs, define curriculum roadmaps and deliver contemporary training programmes. The organisation has evolved to meet the burgeoning training needs of Singaporeans to continuously keep pace with the dynamic business economy.

2008 Global Financial Crisis

The recent global financial crisis, effects of which are still being felt throughout the world, is a good case study of how the labour movement, led by the NTUC and supported by the government, responded by developing retraining schemes and structures to mitigate the effect of job loss and economic restructuring. The impact was primarily felt by professionals, managers, executives and technicians, collectively known as PMETs.

As noted by then Secretary-General of NTUC, Mr Lim Swee Say, "It was the most severe global recession in 70 years and looked set to take the heaviest toll on workers. The International Labour Organisation (ILO) projected that as many as 61 million workers around the world would lose their jobs, driving average world unemployment to above 6.5 per cent.

The very open Singapore economy was not spared. In the first quarter of 2009, the economy contracted by 9.4 per cent. A record 10,900 workers were retrenched, driving unemployment up from 2.5 per cent to 3.3 per cent in just three months. The outlook for the rest of 2009 was just as bleak. The economy was projected to contract by as much as 9 per cent or more for the first year. There was great concern that retrenchment would exceed the 29,000 mark recorded during the Asian financial crisis in 1997–98 — the previous major recession — and quarterly unemployment could surpass the record 4.8 per cent during the SARS (Severe Acute Respiratory Syndrome) health epidemic in 2003.

High employment and volatile global markets appeared to be the "new normal" post 2010. To mitigate this, Singapore's tripartite system comprising employers, labour and government faced its greatest challenge. NTUC had long recognized and advocated that more workers should be armed with developmental skills to take on tomorrow's jobs arising from long-term structural changes. In 1997, it came up with a "skills redevelopment" initiative, providing workers, especially older, less-skilled and less-educated ones, with certifiable skills that were portable and recognised at industry and national levels.

The Skills Redevelopment Programme (SRP) was launched in 1997 to provide certifiable training for about 1,500 rank-and-file workers. The SRP was primarily used to fund absentee-payroll of companies sending their staff for training, as the Skills Development Fund (SDF) was available for paying course fees. Response from companies, unions and workers was encouraging, and the pace picked up even faster when the Asian financial crisis struck Singapore in 1998.

A year later, the SRP received a major funding boost when then Prime Minister Goh Chok Tong, in his address to the tripartite partners at the May Day Rally, announced the government's support for the scheme with a grant of S$50 million. The elevation of the SRP to a national programme was followed by a series of major tripartite and national initiatives including the transformation of the Ministry of Labour into the Ministry of Manpower in 1998; the launch of the National Skills Recognition System (NSRS) in 2000; the setting-up of a multibillion-dollar Lifelong Learning Fund in 2001; the establishment of the Workforce Development Agency (WDA) in 2003 to spearhead the continuing education and training of workers; the introduction of the Employability Skills System in 2004; the revamp of the NSRS into the Workforce Skills Qualification (WSQ) scheme; the launch of the Job Re-creation Programme in 2005; and the establishment of the Employment and Employability Institute in 2008.

One significant and highly innovative initiative of the NTUC came in 2001. Under the Skills Redevelopment Programme (SRP), employees could only receive skills upgrading through employers' sponsorship which resulted in training in their current industries. Therefore, workers in sunset industries were unable to receive help in upgrading themselves to take on new jobs in new industries. Thus, the NTUC-Surrogate Employer Programme (NTUC-SEP) was introduced in October 2001 to help NTUC union members who take responsibility for upgrading their skills without the support of their employers. By acting as the Surrogate Employer (SE), NTUC assisted employed union members to secure SDF training assistance, overcoming one of the constraints of the SRP rules.

With all these adjustments in place, by the time Singapore was hit by the global recession in 2009, the national infrastructure for lifelong learning and enhanced employability was already largely in place and ready to swing into full action to face its most severe test yet.

To mitigate the effects of the crisis on jobs, the government introduced a S$20.5 billion stimulus package, funded by financial reserves. This included a S$4.5 billion Jobs Credit payroll subsidy to encourage companies to retain local workers, and S$650 million under the Skills Programme for Upgrading and Resilience (SPUR) to train and upgrade workers during the downturn.

SPUR-approved courses include all Workforce Skills Qualifications' (WSQ) courses by approved training providers in Human Resource; Healthcare Support; Precision Engineering; Aerospace; Information and Communications Technology; Nitec and Higher Nitec courses for adults under the Institute of Technical Education, e.g. Nitec in Information Technology and Higher Nitec in Electronics Engineering; and Diploma, Advanced Diploma and Specialist Diploma courses for adults provided by the Polytechnics, e.g. Diploma in Technology, Specialist Diploma in Arts & Events Management, Advanced Diploma in Process Control & Instrumentation.

Employability Skills System (ESS)

Introduced by the Workforce Development Agency (WDA) in 2004, the ESS is a set of generic employability skills. These foundational skills, portable across all industries, are aimed to assist workers to adapt to new job demands and changing work environments and create opportunities for upward career movement. The ESS incorporates tools to customize training programmes, ensuring that training is relevant and can be applied at workplaces.

Employment and Employability Institute (e2i)

The Employment and Employability Institute, or e2i, is a concrete manifestation of the strong tripartite way of managing industrial relations in Singapore. An initiative of the NTUC, supported by the WDA, the Singapore Labour Foundation (SLF), and the Singapore National Employers' Federation (SNEF), e2i serves all segments of workers, from the rank and file to professionals, managers and executives. e2i has become the first one-stop centre to help workers raise their employability through career coaching, training, and job matching, while helping employers to recreate and enhance their jobs, upskill and find workers.

Now at the new campus named the Devan Nair Institute of Employment and Employability in honour of the first secretary-general of NTUC and former President of Singapore, e2i is the largest dedicated organisation to creating solutions for better employment and employability. Its mission is to create better jobs and better lives for workers. Since 2008, e2i has helped more than 300,000 workers through providing better jobs, developing better skills through professional development, and improving productivity for companies.

e2i provides expertise in career coaching, skills upgrading, job matching, and developing Place-and-Train programmes to help workers and job seekers make informed choices. e2i also goes upstream to bring career services to schools such as the ITEs and Polytechnics, by linking the students with its extensive network of partnerships with employers and training providers, and help them better understand career options and progressions in the different industries.

It serves both individuals through training for employability, professional development courses as well as job fairs and an employment service. For employers, there are productivity improvement resources, training and job-redesign as well as placement services. e2i is focussed on providing skills upgrading and better jobs for the existing workforce, new job entrants, retrenched workers and career switchers.

There is growing emphasis on the importance of mastery of skills in every job for Singapore to have a bright future. As a focal point for labour movement to help workers upskill and progress, e2i is the primary and de facto intermediary for partners and workers, continuously developing training and job solutions, and working towards jobs that are high-wage and high productivity and growth that is inclusive.

These efforts by the Singapore labour movement to drive training and skills upgrading, supported by different government funding schemes, have complemented pre-employment training by the technical training institutions such as the ITE and Polytechnics. Indeed, these institutions are an integral part of the continuing education system, working closely with employers and the labour movement to ensure that training and upgrading is a part of every person's life. With the SkillsFuture initiative (of which more will be written later), lifelong learning will be a reality for every Singaporean even well past their retirement.

Source: The Singaporean Mid-March 1983. Courtesy of National Trades Union Congress.

Source: Launch of Basic Education for Skills Training (BEST) and Worker Improvement through Secondary Education (WISE) programmes in 1983.

Source: May Day Annual 2001. Courtesy of National Trades Union Congress.

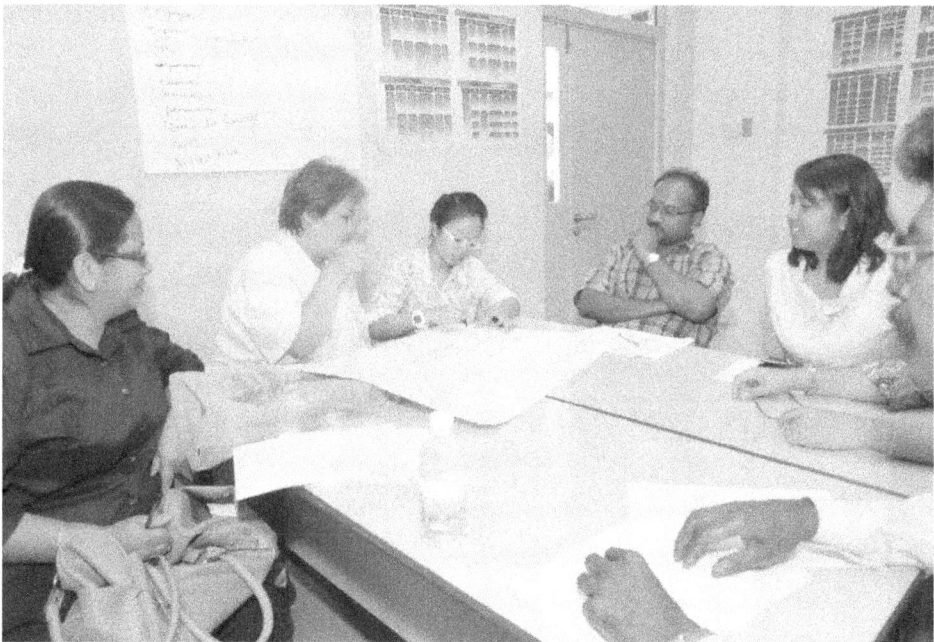

Source: The NTUC this week 17 April 2009. Courtesy of Devan Nair Institute of Employment and Employability.

Source: The NTUC this week 17 April 2009. Courtesy of Devan Nair Institute of Employment and Employability.

Source: Metamorphosis 2010. Courtesy of NTUC Learning Hub.

CHAPTER 8

Connecting TVET with Higher Education

Landmark Events:

1964: Establishment of Singapore Institute of Management (SIM)
1981: Establishment of Nanyang Technological Institute (later NTU)
2005: Establishment of SIM Global Education
2005: Establishment of SIM University (UniSIM)
2009: Establishment of Singapore Institute of Technology (SIT)
2014: Singapore Institute of Technology gazetted as a public university

One of the reasons why vocational and technical education have been accepted in Singapore, apart from quality of training, facilities and employment prospects, is that a system of "bridges and ladders" has been put in place to ensure that vocational training is not a dead-end, but offers multiple options for upgrading and moving up one's career within the same or different discipline.

From Technician to Technologist

Graduates who have obtained the basic Nitec technician qualification can enrol for the next level of Higher Nitec within the ITE system.

Once they have obtained the Higher Nitec certification, they will become eligible to study towards a polytechnic diploma. Many indeed do enter the polytechnics. Students with a Higher Nitec with a GPA greater than 3.5 may be considered for

- Direct entry to 2nd year of relevant 3-year diploma courses, or
- Entry to 1st year of relevant 3-year diploma courses with module exemptions, or

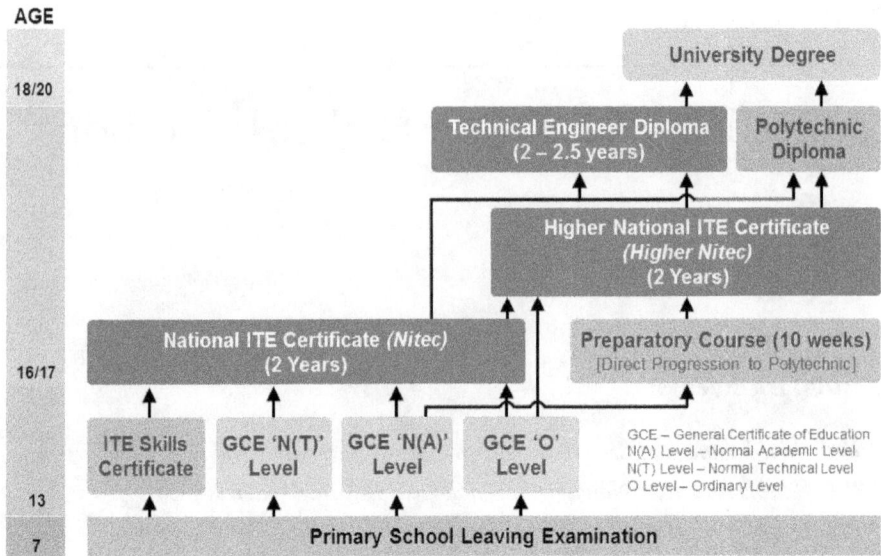

Figure 8.1:   ITE's Progression Pathways

- Entry to 1st year of relevant 3-year diploma courses, or
- Entry to 1st year of relevant 3-year diploma with exemption of 1st 6 months in Year 1

Those whose GPA is between 2.5 and 3.5 will be eligible for entry to 1st year of relevant 3-year diploma courses.

Even those who only have the basic Nitec may qualify to enter the first year of a relevant engineering polytechnic diploma programme, provided they have a GPA of greater than 3.5.

Thus the system is predicated on performance benchmarks that graduates must achieve before being eligible. However even with a GPA of 2.5 and a Higher Nitec certificate, a diploma programme would be available. Since most students would be able to achieve this, the first bridge to a diploma becomes open to them.

In fact, the polytechnics themselves appreciate the practical skills and knowledge that ITE graduates bring to their classrooms and laboratories. They may need some extra coaching in Mathematics and Physics which are now of a higher level, but with coaching from their polytechnic peers and lecturers, most ITE graduates are able to graduate with a polytechnic diploma. All the polytechnics have strong pastoral and academic counselling services for students to turn to and this provides every student with the support they need to keep moving forward to the limits of their own ability.

Advanced Diplomas and Specialist Diplomas

To meet the aspirations of its own graduates for upgrading, the polytechnics created the 2-year Advanced Diploma and 1-year Specialist Diploma routes. As the polytechnics were not degree-granting bodies, this was the furthest they could go. These AD and SD programmes were also open to degree holders who wanted specialised knowledge. Although the numbers were small, these provided an additional option for polytechnic graduates.

However, these post-diploma qualifications did not come with an automatic pay increase or a change in career path that a degree provided, hence their impact was limited. Under SkillsFuture (see Chapter 9), these could be resuscitated to play a more important skill-deepening role.

Upgrading from Diploma to Degree

Polytechnic diploma holders are ambitious and entrepreneurial. As their training has provided them with both hard and soft skills, they are not bounded by their qualifications and aspire to move onwards.

For many years, diploma holders in engineering disciplines found Scottish universities the favoured route to a degree. Universities such as the University of Strathclyde and the University of Glasgow were very popular as the polytechnic grads could obtain an engineering degree with honours after two more years of study. This was possible because of the waiver of two years from the normal four-year engineering degree.

Indeed, this route to an engineering degree qualification was even quicker than the normal route to university through junior college. An engineering degree at a local university was of four years' duration after junior college of two years, a total of six years after O-levels. For the polytechnic diploma holders who went for a Scottish degree, they could get their Honours degree in five years after their O-levels. This was frowned upon by the engineering professional body, as the students coming from junior colleges were deemed to be more academically qualified than the polytechnic graduates. As a result, the Scottish route gradually ran its course and came to an end when other options opened up for polytechnic graduates.

In 1981, the Nanyang Technological Institute (NTI, later to become Nanyang Technological University, or NTU), opened its doors to a practice-oriented engineering education. This opened the doors for polytechnic graduates to obtain their engineering degree locally in three years. When NTI became an autonomous university as NTU, it continued to admit significant numbers of polytechnic graduates into its second year of study, and many such graduates received honours degrees. Over time, one began to read of polytechnic graduates who had achieved Masters and PhD degrees at overseas universities. Such news articles gave hope to many polytechnic diploma holders.

In 1995, the National University of Singapore also created a part-time Bachelor of Technology (B.Tech) programme for polytechnic graduates. Starting with a Bachelors in Electronics Engineering, and currently offering five B.Tech degrees, these were targeted at working technologists so that they need not give up their jobs while studying. Classes are held on evenings and weekends, and could take up to 8 years, but most usually completed their programme in four or five years. Additional preparatory courses were offered to bring the students up to par in Mathematics, Physics and Engineering foundation subjects. However, polytechnic graduates in general felt that admission to full-time study at local universities was challenging due to the limited capacity and high demand for admission from students entering after their GCE A-Levels at the junior colleges.

Other conversion options which were popular with polytechnic graduates were through British and Australian Universities, particularly the latter. In both the UK and Australia, budget cuts for higher education and fee increases saw increased targeted marketing and wooing polytechnic graduates with accommodative policies. This was especially true of many of the newly converted universities in both countries. Australia became a popular destination, mainly because of proximity to Singapore, better weather conditions and the fact that the Australian academic calendar started six months earlier than the UK calendar. Some Australian universities even moved their calendar forward by a few months to cater to these polytechnic graduates.

This articulation route between the Singapore polytechnic diploma and the southern bridge to an Australian degree became the de facto route for many. Exemptions and waivers were provided liberally as well as summer courses to reduce the time and cost of the degree programme. In addition, Australia, especially Perth in the west and Melbourne in the east, had many Singapore migrants, making it a prime university destination.

SIM University (UniSIM) and SIM Global Education

In view of the large numbers of polytechnic graduates going abroad for undergraduate studies, the government implemented several initiatives to provide suitable local opportunities to reduce the outflow.

The Singapore Institute of Management was created in 1964 out of an EDB unit as an autonomous not-for-profit body to develop Singapore's then-scarce supervisory and managerial pool.

The institute began by offering a variety of short courses catering to all levels of management. Subjects included accounting, sales and supervisory skills. Other industry-specific courses and workshops in the early years covered themes on double taxation, the promotion of exports, and tourism.

The aim was to upgrade the competence of managers and executives. SIM also collaborated closely with the then University of Singapore, Nanyang University and Singapore Polytechnic to plan and deliver the courses. The hallmark course was the residential Advanced Management Programme for chief executives and senior management, conducted by professors from Harvard Business School.

Through a grant of $300,000 from the Ford Foundation, SIM played host to postgraduate scholars from the Stanford and Harvard Business Schools in the 1960s. The scholars conducted short courses in finance and marketing, and taught in the Junior Management Programme, the first SIM two-year evening management course that preceded the Diploma in Management Studies.

Diploma in Management Studies

In 1973, SIM launched its first formal management education programme, the Diploma in Management Studies. Gradually the Institute increased its portfolio of courses to include a wide range of Diploma, Bachelor's, Master's and Doctoral programmes in partnership with more than 10 established universities worldwide.

In 1992, SIM was selected by the Ministry of Education to run the Open University Degree Programme to upgrade vernacular teachers in Singapore, and this unit was named the SIM Open University Centre in 2002.

In 2004, SIM initiated a strategic review and what emerged was the reinvention of SIM in 2005 as a multifaceted organisation with three pillars:

1. SIM Society — a not-for-profit membership organisation
2. SIMPL (operating under the brand name of SIM Global Education — a for-profit entity wholly owned by SIM that offers global education locally)
3. SIM University — a not-for-profit degree-awarding private university

SIM GE took over the degree programmes of SIM and today partners more than 10 overseas universities from the US, UK, Europe and Australia which brings together over 70 academic programmes from diploma to master levels.

The development which was highly significant to polytechnic upgraders was the establishment of SIM University (UniSIM) in 2005, conceived as a University for working adults but primarily aimed at polytechnic graduates. It was meant to be a university of second-chance for those who had missed out on university education in their younger days. UniSIM is essentially the private university arm of the Singapore Institute of Management (SIM), and is funded by SIM. As mentioned earlier, the government gave SIM an initial seed fund for the establishment of the Singapore Open University for teacher upgrading. From this humble beginning, UniSIM has grown to become a significant player in the tertiary education landscape with a large number of degree programmes from bachelor degrees to doctorates in a variety of disciplines. The majority of UniSIM's teaching faculty are drawn from business and industry. These "associates" hold full-time jobs but teach part-time in the evenings when the working adults come for classes. This allows UniSIM to tap the experience of the practitioners to make the curriculum more practice-oriented for the students.

More recently, it had been endorsed by government to offer full-time degree programmes, starting with a small cohort of 300 students for three business programmes being offered in 2014 with similar funding support as the autonomous universities. Students taking part-time UniSIM undergraduate programmes also enjoy 55% subsidy of their course fees provided by the government.

There are 5 schools at UniSIM, catering for the wide gamut of requirements. These are:

- School of Arts and Social Sciences
- School of Business
- School of Human Development and Social Services
- School of Science and Technology
- UniSIM College (for full-time programmes)

UniSIM's counterpart, SIM Global Education, partners overseas universities to offer degree programmes under a twinning arrangement. SIM GE was established in 2005 as a private company under the Singapore Institute of Management (SIM). Now it is a profitable powerhouse for SIM and supports the development of UniSIM through regular development grants. SIM GE targets those who wish to have an overseas University degree, and attracts foreign students as well as polytechnic diploma holders.

Together, SIM GE and UniSIM utilise the same campus facilities during the day and evening respectively, helping to lower costs and maximise the use of scarce land assets and infrastructure.

Singapore Institute of Technology (SIT)

The five polytechnics in Singapore, while appreciating the articulation of their generic diplomas into the local universities, were also concerned that many of their specialised diplomas did not fit easily into the offerings of NUS and NTU. They therefore made arrangements with reputed partner overseas universities to establish themselves on campus to offer specialised degrees in niche areas such as Early Childhood Education (Ngee Ann Polytechnic and Wheelock College, USA), Optometry (Singapore Poly and University of Manchester), Culinary Arts (Temasek Poly and the Culinary Institute of America) and Retail Marketing (Nanyang Polytechnic and Stirling University).

These arrangements were supported by the government under the MOE–Foreign Specialised Institution (FSI) scheme.

In 2009, these FSI collaborations in niche areas, which were initiated by the individual polytechnics, came under the unified umbrella of the Singapore Institute of Technology (SIT).

> Quoting from the SIT website: *"The Singapore Institute of Technology (SIT) was established in 2009 to provide more upgrading opportunities for Polytechnic upgraders to obtain industry-focused degrees. Through a unique tripartite collaboration with its overseas university partners and the five local Polytechnics, SIT welcomed its inaugural batch of 500 students enrolled in 10 degree programmes offered by 5 overseas university partners in September 2010".*

In 2012, the Committee on University Education Pathways Beyond 2015 (CUEP) recommended that SIT be developed into Singapore's fifth Autonomous University (AU), with the authority to issue its own degrees. SIT's goal was to produce a different breed of graduate to meet the diverse needs of Singapore's economy using the applied pathway as its pedagogical foundation.

By integrating theory with hands-on application, students will be exposed to real-life work environments, thereby training them to be work-ready upon graduation. This suits the polytechnic upgraders very well and keeps them focused on the same discipline as their earlier diploma. SIT hopes that using the applied pathway model, it can develop individuals who build on their existing foundation and talents together with its university partners.

In March 2014, the SIT Act was gazetted and passed into legislation, officially making SIT Singapore's newest autonomous university. Together with students enrolling into the degree programmes offered by its overseas university partners, SIT welcomed its inaugural cohort of students for its own degree programmes in Academic Year 2014.

SIT has opened branch campuses in all the five polytechnics, thus making it even easier for polytechnic graduates to find something suitable. In addition to the programmes of its partners, SIT has also developed its own suite of undergraduate degree programmes offered at its HQ campus and will expand these over time. Therefore SIT became another popular option for polytechnic upgraders and as its facilities and offerings grow, could compete with UniSIM for students.

Twinning Programmes with PEIs

About 45% of each post-secondary cohort enters the polytechnic sector, together with 25% into the ITE sector. Thus the diploma and degree upgrading route is a very lucrative one for private education providers. A large number of private educational institutions (PEIs) have therefore emerged over the past 10–15 years to tap this market. Almost every tier 2 and tier 3 university from the UK and Australia has a presence in the marketplace offering their degree programmes through local players.

The biggest players on the scene are SIM Global, Kaplan Singapore, MDIS, PSB Academy, EASB, MIS, Informatics Academy, ERC Institute and many others. Most offer degrees in Business, Commerce, Tourism, Hospitality and ICT, although there are some which also offer lab-based programmes as well.

These PEIs come under the regulatory authority of the Council for Private Education (CPE), which ensures that there are no misleading advertisements, that student fees are protected, that courses are conducted as promised in facilities that are regularly inspected. A CPE Student Services Centre ensures that students, many of whom are from overseas, have the opportunity to register their complaints and have them investigated. The enforcement arm of CPE is well-regarded and feared and some PEIs have been shuttered by the CPE for non-performance. This is to protect Singapore's reputation for high standards and to prevent a laissez-faire market in education. The CPE's EduTrust certification is a much-desired mark of quality that PEIs can aspire to.

Branch Campuses of Overseas Universities

Some overseas universities have established branch campuses of their own in Singapore, for undergraduate as well as postgraduate studies. These too offer an upgrading path for polytechnic graduates. Among the more successful ones are James Cook University (JCU) of Australia, the University of Nevada Las Vegas (UNLV) and Curtin University.

Evolution of the Tertiary Education Landscape

As can be seen, the tertiary education landscape in Singapore is very varied and diversified. Almost anyone with a polytechnic diploma or 12 years of schooling will find a university or college that will admit him or her. This is an issue of concern for the government as graduate unemployment is a serious issue in many developed countries where economic growth has slowed down or turned negative. The past growth rates of the Singapore economy are unlikely to be repeated due to the maturing of the economy into a high-wage, high-value added economy competing at the highest levels globally.

As global markets will remain subdued for some time, and Singapore's growth rates are in the low single digits, it is a dangerous development that an undergraduate degree has become the base qualification for all school leavers. To address the quality issue, government has stepped up support for UniSIM and SIT. To address the quantity issue, government has announced various initiatives under SkillsFuture, to allow for a more orderly individual upgrading plan commensurate with economic growth, based on deepening knowledge and skills, and re-skilling rather than on an unabated chase for a paper qualification. This is discussed in detail in the next chapter.

CHAPTER 9

Preparing for a Skills-Based Future

> **Landmark Events:**
>
> *January 2014: Establishment of the ASPIRE Committee by MOE*
> *August 2014: Publication of ASPIRE Report and Parliamentary debate*
> *August 2014: Announcement of Skills Future Initiative*

As higher education, marked by the acquisition of a degree, becomes a benchmark for an educated society and a knowledge-based economy, mass higher education has become the norm in developed countries and the goal for developing economies. More recently however, the long-standing correlation between earnings and higher education has been severely dented by high graduate unemployment in many countries. This has led many policy-makers to re-examine some fundamental assumptions regarding higher education.

Two broad conclusions have been generally propounded in recent studies. First, that higher education needs to re-emphasise STEM, or Science, Technology, Engineering and Maths studies. A shift away from STEM disciplines towards business, humanities and general education has resulted in lower employability among graduates. Although there are still many proponents of a broader liberal education as a foundation for personal development and growth, policy-makers are concerned with the fall in enrolments in STEM disciplines as these are seen as essential to growth, development and innovation and to solve the problems of the future.

A second conclusion is that any form of higher education must come together with a skill. For example, in addition to knowing about and understanding big data, one must have a strong data analytics background and relevant skills. With the drop in STEM enrolments, there could be a situation of too many generalists vying for too few positions, with too few specialists to fill demand. Part of the reason is that many skills have been outsourced from the high-cost economies to low-cost economies, mainly for cost reasons, but also due to a shortage of skills. Furthermore, those with basic skills have to go for further training to deepen skills, to a level that can keep the person in gainful and productive employment regardless of economic cycles.

In the developing world, there is also an increasing realisation that there has been insufficient investment in vocational and technical training, in favour of university education. This is true throughout Asia, Africa and the Middle East. Countries which have developed their vocational and technical education (VTE) systems have had higher rates of growth sustained over many years. They also have lower levels of youth unemployment and greater social stability.

These lessons have not been lost on Singapore's policy-makers and planners. Even with an excellent TVET system in place, a university education is still the final goal of many parents for their children, even if it means getting degrees from less-reputed universities. This can result in not enough people doing the jobs requiring skills. At the same time, there is also the need to allow everyone to be educated to their maximum potential.

This conundrum led the Ministry of Education (MOE) in January 2014 to establish the Applied Study in Polytechnics and ITE Review (or ASPIRE) Committee. ASPIRE was an apt acronym as the committee would be considering the aspirations of the students in these institutions as well as the nation as a whole. Its Chairperson was Ms Indranee Rajah, then Senior Minister of State, Ministry of Law and Ministry of Education, and its members comprised prominent stake-holders in industry, community, public service and academia.

The ASPIRE study focused on three key areas, as follows:

Strengthening Applied Pedagogy and Industry Links

This group would study and recommend strategies to strengthen the applied education pathways, in partnership with industry, to enhance career and academic progression for Polytechnic and ITE graduates.

Enhancing Student Success

This group would study and recommend strategies to better match students' strengths and interests to applied education pathways and opportunities, and examine supporting mechanisms to increase their chances of success.

Strengthening Research, Innovation and Enterprise

This group would study and recommend strategies to enhance collaboration between polytechnics/ITE and industry in industrial research, innovation and enterprise (RIE) to raise the currency and effectiveness of teaching and learning, and allow the polytechnics and ITE to contribute more directly to industry and the knowledge economy through RIE activities that also support their academic mission.

The ASPIRE study recognised that the demand for workplace skills and competencies would evolve as Singapore's economic environment became more dynamic, varied and complex. It would be necessary to prepare and empower Polytechnic and ITE graduates to seize the opportunities and thrive in the economy of the future.

Issues Addressed by the ASPIRE Committee

First, due to higher aspirations, there appeared to be a trend in graduates going for paper qualifications. Employer feedback was that graduates wanted to move up in their careers too fast, without really getting their hands dirty. They wanted to be in supervisory or management positions relatively quickly and soon after graduation.

Second, the approach to technical education must help ensure that polytechnic and ITE students continue to be well equipped for work and life even as the operating environment evolved. There was a need to look into whether there was a match between industry needs and student qualifications, skills and capabilities.

Third, there were insufficient local employees in the technical and engineering arenas and a high outflow to other careers. There was an over-dependency on foreign labour, especially in the manufacturing sector. The industry would have a big role to play in this aspect by ensuring employability and job relevance, and providing learning on-the-job.

Last but not least, lifelong learning should not be just about getting higher qualifications, but developing deeper knowledge and skills to be better at the job. It would take a generation or more to recalibrate the notion of ability, from grades to knowledge and skills, as it would require a cultural change of how people were valued and a shift in mindset and paradigm. While employers would be key in bringing about such a change by giving better status, pay and recognition to skilled workers and craftsmen, it would also have to start in schools through applied learning.

Mr Bruce Poh, Director and CEO of ITE, observed some trends among trained graduates, despite the fact that 90% of ITE and polytechnic graduates found jobs within 6 months of graduation.

"One trend is an increasing number of students desiring a college degree. This is especially true, as more families are becoming more affluent and aspirations are very high.

In Asian societies, people revere getting a degree, but if done to the extreme there are issues. For example, in Taiwan, more than 90% have a degree and many people are under- or unemployed. Even if there is full employment, people are still pursuing paper qualifications.

Another trend is that people are not going into employment right away after polytechnic; instead, they pursue another diploma.

And a third trend is that people train for a particular area and then switch to another sector.

Finally, industry is always changing so it is no longer the case that it is possible to be trained for life; throughout life, you need to reinvent yourself and possibly change careers."

The ASPIRE Recommendations

After actively engaging key stakeholders, including students, parents, educators and staff in polytechnics, ITE and schools, and employers, the ASPIRE Committee released its report. In it were the following 10 recommendations, covering 4 broad themes:

Theme 1: Helping students make well-informed education and career choices

This theme focussed on empowering Singapore youths to make well-informed decisions for their future. Accurate and current information should be given to them so that they would be able to make good choices about their education and careers. This should also be the case for working adults.

Under this theme, the following recommendation was made

- To strengthen education and career guidance efforts in schools, polytechnics and ITE.

Theme 2: Strengthening education and training in polytechnics and ITE

This theme covered the provision of strong applied education and a strong skills foundation that were deemed to be the hallmarks of the polytechnics and ITE.

It also included the extension of adequate support to help every student succeed in his or her studies.

Accordingly, these were the recommendations:

- To enhance internships at the polytechnics and ITE;
- To increase the progression opportunities from Nitec to Higher Nitec so ITE graduates can deepen their skills;
- To establish polytechnic and ITE leads for each key industry sector to strengthen linkages with industry and help enhance programme offerings;
- To expand online learning opportunities to make it easier for individuals to learn anywhere and anytime;
- To provide more development and support programmes for polytechnic and ITE students to help every enrolled student succeed.

Theme 3: Helping polytechnic and ITE students deepen skills post-graduation

This theme delved into the provision of more avenues for polytechnic and ITE graduates to deepen existing skills or acquire new ones. In addition, it examined how to better bridge the transition from school to work, enable youths to apply the skills acquired and build upon them further in their jobs.

The recommendations were as follows:

- To launch new programmes that integrate work and study, such as place-and-train (later renamed as 'Earn and Learn' under SkillsFuture) programmes, to provide an additional skills-upgrading option for polytechnic and ITE graduates;
- To increase post-diploma Continuing Education and Training opportunities at polytechnics to refresh and deepen the skills of polytechnic graduates;
- To support vocation-based deployments during National Service (NS) to help polytechnic and ITE graduates maintain and hone their skills, and perhaps obtain industry-recognised accreditation that will enable them to be better placed to join the industry they had trained for, upon completing NS.

Theme 4: Helping polytechnic and ITE graduates progress in their careers

This theme looked into progression pathways and skills frameworks that could also serve as benchmarks for hiring and progression practices within the industry.

The recommendation was:

- To develop sector-specific skills frameworks and career progression pathways in collaboration with industry to support progression based on industry-relevant skills.

Considerations in Response to the ASPIRE Report

The ASPIRE Report was much discussed in Parliament. Ministers and Members of Parliament, while endorsing the recommendations, also brought up several other key considerations:

- Having a holistic approach to the post-secondary education landscape;
- Sending conflicting messages regarding degree versus non-degree qualifications;
- Encouraging recognition for performance at work instead of looking primarily at paper qualifications;
- Getting industry and employers to be on board and changing their mindset.

In addressing these concerns during the Parliamentary debate, ASPIRE Review Chairman, Ms Indranee Rajah, highlighted that ASPIRE was part of a bigger, holistic, strategic move by the Government. The primary and secondary schools would first lay a strong academic foundation. In addition, the Applied Learning Programme would focus on the application of skills in the real world, taught through problem solving, supporting tie-ups with industry partners; the Learning for Life Programme would concentrate on real-world experiential learning to develop character and values through community outreach programmes or service learning projects.

At the university level, an applied degree pathway, with an emphasis on learning through work and industry, was being offered at the Singapore Institute of Technology (SIT) and SIM University, with other universities like the National University of Singapore and Nanyang Technological University also looking into strengthening partnerships with industry and internships. ASPIRE's focus was deeper applied learning at the polytechnic and ITE levels, to complete the whole spectrum and to create an impact beyond these institutions.

Ms Rajah further explained that career guidance efforts would adopt a whole-life approach, starting at primary through secondary levels, and going though the polytechnics and ITE, and universities, as well as on to working adults who will be guided to progress in their careers through sector-specific skills frameworks. To this end, the polytechnics and ITE would develop a new education and career guidance programme covering areas such as personal management and career exploration.

This would be an important area of focus for the ITE and polytechnics, unlike in Switzerland, where intermediary organisations play a big part in baseline training and career development. The lack of a tradition of apprenticeship in Singapore does little to anchor graduates to a specific domain area of expertise.

Instead, they tend to move from domain to domain without deepening their skills. Hence, early career guidance would be a useful intervention.

School teachers and parents also need play a part in this effort. To this end, career counsellors are being recruited for secondary schools, and this will be done for ITE and the polytechnics too. They will undergo extensive and ongoing training so that they will have a realistic understanding of the economy and careers available. Companies would also be involved in making available current information and hosting student visits. Parent education on what would be in store for their children in industry would also be stepped up.

On the issue of conflicting signals or messaging on degree versus non-degree qualifications as well as recognition of performance rather than just paper qualifications, excerpts of Education Minister Mr Heng Swee Keat's speech in Mandarin during the Parliamentary debate provides insights on how the government was looking to address this.

> *"… the objective of ASPIRE is for us to break away from our customary thinking about qualifications, career and opportunities. There are three breakthroughs that we seek. The first is to go beyond qualifications to recognise the attitude, deep skills, knowledge and experience that enable us to perform and excel. The second is to go beyond the classroom to learn continuously, recognise the value of applied learning and lifelong learning, and make the workplace a learning place. This is where employers play an important role in developing people. The third is to go beyond narrow definitions of success to recognise that everyone excels at different things, in different ways, and that we can all excel if we apply our minds, hands, and hearts to what we do."*
>
> *None of these breakthroughs devalues some qualifications over others. It is not about one kind of qualification versus another. It is about creating more opportunities, opening up more pathways so that everyone can excel and succeed."*

Taking the lead a few months later, the Public Service Division (PSD) announced that there would be faster career progression for the non-graduate Management Support Officers who demonstrate the required performance and capability. The Civil Service also announced that it would merge more of what used to be separate graduate schemes of service into integrated schemes in which, regardless of the starting point, officers could progress according to their performance and ability to handle larger responsibilities.

Ms Rajah also addressed strategies for getting industry and employers on board and changing their mindset. This was likely be a challenge for businesses, especially SMEs, because of costs and manpower issues. However, there were government grants that they could tap into and benefits that they would gain from building up progressive pathways, providing training programmes, and developing good human resources for building up their manpower development capabilities. The former includes SPRING's Capability Development Grant and SME Talent Programme as well as the Workforce Development Agency's Enterprise Training Support.

Ms Rajah also acknowledged that changing current, deeply entrenched mindsets would be challenging. She observed in her speech:

"One noteworthy thing is that everybody in this House who has spoken on this has not just pointed out the need for the mindset change, but agrees that it should be changed. So, you can see that there is strong support, even in this Chamber. When we speak to others, many agree that there is a need for it. That is a good starting point because if people recognise that this is something which needs to be changed — and they think it is a good thing to be changed — then it is really a question of everybody doing his or her own part and taking it on board. For individuals — to recognise our strengths, to build on the right foundations, choose the right paths, and adopt the right attitude to lifelong learning. For parents — realise your child's unique strengths and encourage him or her on the path that will best develop his or her talent. For employers — value every employee, hire and reward based on actual skills."

In addition, she called for Singaporeans to take on a broad definition of success, and to celebrate and support individuals who strive and do well, be it those who trod a non-traditional path to achieve success in their own ways as well as those who have done so via the degree route. Similarly, she urged for recognition for companies who espoused the right mindsets. These would include companies that invest in their people, education and training; hire, remunerate and promote based on actual skills and performance; take on sector-specific skills frameworks and progression pathways; and continually improve jobs and progression opportunities for their employees.

Ms Rajah also emphasised that, while the ASPIRE Committee gained insights from their visits to many countries, the recommendations made were uniquely Singaporean.

Excerpts taken from her speech sum up what ASPIRE aimed to achieve.

"ASPIRE seeks to be a game changer. We are trying to realign education with industry to cope with a new environment. We are making a strategic course adjustment. The previous course was right for that time, but we are setting a new course because once

again, the winds of change are upon us. We must tack to a new wind. If we do not make the change, it will be forced upon us and not on our terms.

We are making a societal change, to go beyond qualifications, to go beyond the class-room, to go beyond narrow definitions of success. Some may say that these are lofty goals, high ideals, but how will we actually implement them? ... It is not an easy task. It will not happen overnight. It will take many years, but the journey of a thousand miles begins with a single step. ASPIRE is that step.

This is the beginning, but it is just that — only the beginning. Now we need everyone else to start making the necessary concrete changes in their own areas.

It is like turning a ship. You turn the ship's wheel, the gears engage. You are fighting against the water resistance. The ship slowly starts to move, and the initial move takes an awful lot of effort. But then it gains momentum and you start to pick up speed, and then you are full steam ahead. This is what the ASPIRE effort is like.

We are contemplating the horizon, trying to figure out what is to come, anticipating as best we can, coming up with solutions and strategies, and then doing it together in a concerted effort. That is a very Singaporean thing; it is a very Singaporean approach. We are doing this for one reason and one reason only — to secure a better future for Singaporeans and Singapore."

The Government accepted the ASPIRE Committee's recommendations. The new reforms signalled "a watershed in the education landscape", and a move away from the traditional approach of frontloading education via pre-employment training to having an emphasis on more continuing education and training pro-grammes. One of the challenges would be in changing tradition towards having an apprenticeship-style education. Singapore could adapt the European appren-ticeship model while keeping full-time vocational education. Apprenticeship schemes would address the issue of students not completing a course, then later starting another upon completion of national service. Apprenticeship during national service would pave the way for deeper skills development. Another rea-son was that, by bringing education, manpower, employment, and training all together, it would accomplish higher productivity and more innovation, especially as skills need changing rapidly in this present age.

In August 2014, in his National Day Rally speech, Singapore Prime Minister Lee Hsien Loong announced the setting up of the SkillsFuture Council, which would take over the implementation of the recommendations made by the ASPIRE Committee. Besides the ASPIRE recommendations, the Council would also be supported by the Continuing Education and Training (CET)

Masterplan, to realise the nation's vision of a future based on skills and mastery. Hence an understanding of the CET Masterplan is also key to understanding SkillsFuture.

The Continuing Education and Training (CET) Masterplan

The CET Masterplan or CET 2020 was developed by the Singapore Workforce Development Agency (WDA), with feedback from individuals, unions and employers and after identifying major shifts that would be needed to enable Singaporeans to be career-resilient in an advanced economy driven by innovation and productivity. The plan focussed on changing key relationships with employers, individuals and training providers.

CET 2020's key strategies are:

Increased Involvement by Employers in Building and Valuing Skills
The end result of this strategy would be to enable individuals to deepen their professional competencies, and based on skills gained, advance in their careers.

Specific initiatives include:

- Working closely with sector lead agencies, employers and unions to co-develop manpower and skills strategies to support industry growth and productivity efforts. Sector-specific manpower and skills requirements over a five-year period would be identified and a holistic package of measures to meet these would be outlined.
- Building on the existing Singapore Workforce Skills Qualifications (WSQ) frameworks to develop sectoral competency frameworks that will underpin the development of pre-employment training programmes offered by the polytechnics and ITE, as well as CET programmes. These frameworks will guide human resource practices such as recruiting and planning career progression pathways for employees, as well as enable individuals to better understand how they can deepen their skills in specific sectors and progress in their careers.
- Stepping up efforts to reach out to SMEs to offer manpower and training advisory support and facilitate their access to government schemes that address their needs in these areas. This aims to increase the proportion of SMEs that provided structured training and development for their employees. In 2012, the proportion was 68%, lower than the overall average of 71%, and was a cause for concern as SMEs employed 70% of the total workforce.

Enable Individuals to make Informed Learning and Career Choices through Improved Delivery of Education, Training and Career Guidance

The focus was to make available resources and tools that would help individuals to discover their strengths and interests, coupled with relevant labour information that would enable them to make informed education, training and career choices.

Specific initiatives include:

- Partnering with MOE to develop an integrated education, training and career guidance online portal. Beginning with their journey in schools and lasting throughout their careers, the portal will allow individuals to chart and review their education, training and career developments. A prototype Individual Learning Portfolio had already been piloted with 18,000 users earlier in 2014 and feedback gathered from them would be incorporated in the design of the national portal.
- Establishing a Lifelong Learning Exploration Centre at the Lifelong Learning Institute (LLI) for visitors to learn more about themselves through profiling tests and games and explore learning pathways that can help them fulfil their career aspirations.
- Increasing the pool of WDA's career coaches and raising the professional competencies of the current ones in delivering education, training and career guidance, particularly in providing support to different workforce segments.

Wide Range of High-Quality Learning Opportunities in a Vibrant CET Ecosystem

The focus for this strategy would be to raise the overall quality of training providers, adult educators and training programmes. The polytechnics and ITE would be roped in to step up their CET for working adults, along with high-quality private CET providers.

Key initiatives include:

- Introduction of more blended learning courses that combine classroom and online learning as well as more engaging and accessible e-learning. The WDA's Institute for Adult Learning would take the lead to experiment with and innovate in using technology to deliver training, and share its learning and insights with CET partners.
- Setting up an iN.LAB at the Lifelong Learning Institute, which would supply a conducive, creative environment in which CET partners and practitioners

could collaborate, experiment, apply and invent innovative pedagogical as well as cutting-edge learning solutions.

- Introducing more structured workplace-based learning, in authentic learning environments, which enable trainees to apply the skills acquired immediately. This would see WDA working with training providers, sector lead agencies and industry to establish more Place-and-Train programmes, including those targeted at fresh polytechnic and ITE graduates.

The ASPIRE Report and the CET Masterplan 2020, taken together, represent the future of the technical and skills landscape of the future. No documentation of the past 50 years of technical education would be complete without a final laying out of what Singapore is trying to achieve in the next 20 years. This would be as revolutionary and cutting-edge in concept and implementation as the transformation of the TVET sector in between 1995 and 2015.

SkillsFuture

The ASPIRE Report and CET 2020 led to the setting up of a tripartite SkillsFuture Council, announced by no less than Prime Minister Lee Hsien Loong during the August 2014 National Day Rally. Chaired by Deputy Prime Minister and then Minister for Finance, Mr Tharman Shanmugaratnam, the Council comprises 25 representatives from diverse stakeholder sectors that included the government, industry, unions and employers, and educational and training institutions. Its role — to drive a major, long-term national effort to develop skills for the future and help Singaporeans develop a future based on skills mastery.

The Council's vision was articulated by Mr Shanmugaratnam as follows:

"In our next wave of development, we will build a first-rate system of continuing education and training: learning throughout life. It will intertwine education and the world of work in ways that strengthen and enrich both. It will make the workplace a major site of learning. It will enable every Singaporean to maximise his or her potential, from young and through life. It will build an advanced economy and ensure us of a fair society."

SkillsFuture signals the start of a major mindset shift. Positioned as a national movement, it looks at broader definition of success, one that is not limited by grades linked only to academic achievements. It aims to create a culture where every job is respected and rewarded. It encourages Singaporeans to continually strive towards greater excellence through knowledge, application and experience, and to go beyond learning for grades to learning for mastery.

As a start, the SkillsFuture Council will focus on four main areas.

- *Helping individuals to make well-informed choices in education, training and careers*
  This would involve the development of a full system of guidance to help individuals make choices in education, training and their careers, starting from educational counselling in schools and extending throughout a person's working life. Collaboration between the Government, industry, and institutions will be fostered to provide individuals with exposure to a wide range of occupations and industries from young and ongoing information on the changing needs of the labour market.
- *Developing an integrated, high-quality system of education and training that responds to constantly evolving industry needs*
  This strategy would involve an education and training review to ensure that a sound and broad-based education for the young is complemented with a full menu of continuous learning options, including opportunities to develop new specialisations.
- *Promoting employer recognition and career development based on skills and mastery*
  This would see employers being roped in to design and implement a framework that would enable individuals to advance by climbing skill ladders.
- *Fostering a culture that supports and celebrates lifelong learning*
  This would involve a long-term effort to respect every job for its skills, and value the achievements of individuals who attain mastery in their own fields. The habit of learning throughout life, for work as well as for interest, would also be promoted.

Specific programmes and initiatives of the Council in the next few years have been spelt out on its official website and are indicated in the following paragraphs:

Developing Sectoral Manpower Plans (SMPs)

This will see employers, unions, education and training providers, trade associations and the Government joining forces to identify current and future skills needs for specific sectors and set out a systematic plan to develop these in the local workforce. Each SMP will take into account the outlook of the sector, its future development, and the manpower and skills needed, including new ones that can arise as a result of technology advancements and other macro driving forces. It will articulate and develop clear career progression pathways that will be closely integrated with education, training and development, to ensure greater fluidity between learning and working. The SMPs will also lay out plans to attract, retain and develop a deep pool of talent in the sector.

For a start, the SMPs will focus on sectors that have more pressing manpower needs such as healthcare, early childhood care and education, and social services. New growth ones such as biopharmaceuticals that provide exciting job opportunities and require a larger pipeline of workers as well as those that are facing significant manpower challenges, like retail and food services, will also be focused on.

Strengthening Education and Career Guidance

A more structured and comprehensive Education and Career Guidance (ECG) system will be put in place to support individuals at different life stages, with MOE and WDA coordinating national efforts across public sector agencies and in collaboration with industry partners. From 2015 onwards, first-year students will receive systematic ECG with a minimum duration of 40–60 hours across two years in the ITE and three years in polytechnics. The content will focus on helping students develop skills to make career choices and transit from schools to the workplace. Learning objectives will be incorporated into existing academic modules and dedicated lessons on career-related topics. There will also be out-of-classroom activities including industry immersion programmes, talks, workshops, and individual and group career guidance sessions. The local universities will also be establishing closer links with industry professionals and enhancing their existing career services to equip students with greater occupational and industry knowledge.

Thus, more ECG counsellors will be recruited and trained. Close to 100 ECG Counsellors will be needed so as to have six at each polytechnic and ITE college and one assigned to every five secondary schools/Junior Colleges/Centralised Institute. Besides working with schools, polytechnics and the ITE, these counsellors will establish partnerships with industries and government agencies to obtain information on the labour market and industry trends, as well as study and career options.

WDA will continue to tailor its career and training advisory services to the needs of different workforce segments, either through personalised services at the WDA Career Centres and CaliberLink, or through more self-help career resources, such as the Jobs Bank (www.jobsbank.gov.sg), and the Tripartite Career Resource

Portal (www.careerresource.sg) which provides resources to individuals to strengthen their career development.

Therefore, ECG practitioners will need to be equipped with the necessary career counselling, guidance and advisory capabilities and opportunities to deepen their skills. Structured and accredited training programmes will be put in place for them.

To support the ECG efforts, there will be a one-stop online portal, rolled out in phases from 2017, offering customised profiling and assessment tools and resources, as well as information on the education, training and career options available to individuals at different life stages. This Individual Learning Portfolio (ILP) portal will enable individuals to take charge of their career and lifelong learning by providing them with a better understanding of their own strengths and interests, through online psychometric and skills inventory assessment tools. These tools will assist individuals in understanding their work interests, skills confidence and work values, facilitating exploration and decision-making. There will be intelligent job matching and training recommender functions that link individuals to the relevant types of industries and occupations as well as jobs available via a Jobs Bank. The portal will also hold a repository of self-help articles, labour market information and Government subsidised training courses to help users decide whether they should stay in an industry, change occupations or re-skill themselves to enter a new or adjacent field.

Strengthening Students' Learning Experiences

School Directors and Course Managers will make enhancements to internships for two-thirds of all polytechnic courses and half of all ITE courses over the next two years, and for all ITE and polytechnic courses by 2020. These enhancements include establishing defined learning outcomes and supporting structured activities during the internship. This may mean curriculum adjustments to allow better integration of internships with classroom learning, longer internship durations to support better learning and skills application as well as customisation to meet the needs of the host companies. The local universities will also be continually aligning their programmes with industry needs via both curricula and internships.

A SkillsFuture Earn and Learn Programme was also launched in March 2015. In the work-study programme, fresh graduates from polytechnics and ITE will be matched to suitable employers related to their disciplines of study. They will undergo structured on-the-job training and mentorship, and have a hand in company projects, thereby deepening skills acquired in school. Participating employers will benefit by being able to easily recruit local fresh talent and prepare them for work within the organisation, while participants can look forward to industry-recognised certification, a competitive starting salary and sign-on incentive of $5000, and a structured career development pathway in the company.

As of end March 2015, 61 employers had signed up for the programme, offering close to 150 places in eight sectors such as food services, games development, logistics, infocomm technology, marine and offshore engineering, retail, and precision engineering. It aims to eventually cover up to one in three polytechnic and ITE graduates.

To enable more students to have an international immersion experience that better prepares them for future global careers, the *Young Talent Programme*, which currently subsidises only students from local universities, will be extended to all polytechnics and the ITE.

Providing Study Subsidies and Awards

A SkillsFuture Jubilee Fund to kickstart support for the SkillsFuture movement and to mark the celebration of Singapore's 50 years of independence (SG50) will be established. The Fund will comprise donations from employers, unions, and the public, with the Government providing a dollar for dollar matching grant for donations raised. It will be utilised for SkillsFuture Fellowships, to recognise and develop Singaporeans with deep skills acquired through significant work experience in the same industry/occupation. Each Fellowship comprises a cash award of $10,000 to support recipients in achieving skills mastery in their respective fields. Award recipients must have had a strong track record of contributing to the skills development of others, which they are expected to maintain. They will form a group of 'Fellows' who will be role models in the pursuit of skills mastery. A hundred fellowships will be given out annually from 2016 onwards.

Non-monetary SkillsFuture Employer Awards will also be given out to exemplary employers who have made significant efforts to invest in employee training and support the SkillsFuture effort through the development of structured skills-based career pathways for their employees.

A SkillsFuture account has been created for every citizen aged 25 and above to tap into, to deepen their skills in existing fields and broaden their horizon in areas outside their current fields. Each citizen will receive an initial credit of $500, with further top-ups made annually. Subsequent cohorts who turn 25 would similarly receive an initial credit of $500. To be used to offset course fees (only for education and training initiated by the individuals themselves), these credits would not expire. The courses will include those subsidised by the WDA, those offered by MOE-funded tertiary institutions including polytechnics and ITE, and selected ones at SIM University, LASALLE College of the Arts, and Nanyang Academy of Fine Arts. Courses supported by other public agencies will be added further down the road.

A SkillsFuture Study Award of up to $5000 will also be made available to support individuals, especially those in the early to mid stages of their careers, to develop and deepen specialist skills needed by future economic growth sectors and those meeting social needs. It will also support individuals with deep specialist skills to develop other competencies such as business and cross-cultural skills. For starters, the awards will cover sectors such as advanced manufacturing, next generation logistics, healthcare, and financial services. A maximum of 2000 awards annually would be given out in the medium term, in phases.

To help mid-career Singaporeans to up-skill and re-skill to stay responsive to a changing workplace, there will be more skills-based modular courses made available at post-secondary education institutions. These will be targeted at the diploma, post-diploma and undergraduate levels. Working adults will be able to acquire relevant skills without having to go for a full qualification; however, they can also combine several modules to get a full qualification. By the end of 2015, there will be over 300 modular courses offered by polytechnics and universities, in specialist areas such as Digital Forensics and Investigation, Naval Architecture and Marine Engineering, Functional Genomics and Coaching and Counselling Skills.

Subsidies will also be made available, from October 2015 onwards, for these mid-career individuals who may face more opportunity costs and competing demands in the form of job and family commitments in undertaking training. Those aged 40 and above will enjoy higher subsidies of at least 90% of programme costs for MOE-funded courses and up to 90% of course fees for WDA-supported courses.

Supporting SMEs

To help SMEs cope with the constant challenge of recruiting and retaining talent, and to ensure that local professionals, managers and executives (PMEs), who will form the majority of the workforce in the future, stay gainfully employed within SMEs, a programme called P-Max has been created. Under P-Max, Programme Managers, namely the Association of Small and Medium Enterprises (ASME) and the Singapore National Employers Federation (SNEF), would administer Place-and-Train (PnT) programmes for SMEs and PMEs. These programmes aim to screen and place job-seeking PMEs into suitable SME jobs and help SMEs to better recruit, train, manage and retain their newly hired PMEs as well as encourage them to adopt progressive human resource practices.

To facilitate this, both SME representatives and their newly-hired PMEs would be required to attend workshops, the fees of which will be 90% funded by WDA. They would then be followed up six months later when SMEs who retained their newly-hired PME employee would be eligible for a one-off S$5,000 Assistance Grant.

Cultivating Mentors and Leaders

SPRING Singapore, a government agency to promote small and medium businesses, will work with partners in key sectors to build up a pool of SkillsFuture mentors who will help SMEs develop the potential of their workforce.

These mentors would include retirees with deep skills and experience, and mid-career professionals and executives with experience and know-how in different fields. They will help SMEs implement measures to deepen the skills of their workforce and help their supervisors and managers to develop coaching skills. To recruit and manage these mentors and match them to interested SMEs, SPRING Singapore will appoint industry partners such as Trade Associations and Chambers and Centres of Innovation. This process will start in the third quarter of 2015, with the aim to have a pool of 200 mentors in the next two years.

A SkillsFuture Leadership Development Initiative is also in the pipeline. This will support aspiring Singaporeans in developing the necessary capabilities to take on increased roles and responsibilities in their respective companies. These individuals, while having the necessary work experience and competencies, will also need to be exposed to key global or regional markets and critical business functions. To enable this, the government will support companies keen to create and/or enhance in-house programmes that may include overseas assignments to key markets and cross-functional rotations. It will also work with industry, Institutes of Higher Learning, and companies to make available relevant, quality leadership and managerial development courses and programmes.

Encouraging Innovation in Training

As mentioned earlier, an Innovation Lab known as iN.LAB will be set up by the WDA's Institute for Adult Learning (IAL). iN.LAB will provide a conducive environment to support CET partners and practitioners in their efforts to cultivate collaboration and experimentation, build capabilities and establish networks to develop innovative training and learning solutions that would benefit learners and the CET Community.

SkillsFuture was hotly discussed during the 2015 Budget Debate. Ministers and Members of Parliament, while strongly supporting SkillsFuture, were also concerned that for it to succeed, policy alone would not suffice. Employers committed to staff training and development, individuals who will take greater ownership over their own growth, and a quantum leap in mindset change among all stakeholders — these would be critical towards its success.

In addressing many of the issues that surfaced, Education Minister Mr Heng Swee Keat outlined three major shifts on the horizon which he termed "Learning for mastery, Learning throughout life, Learning for life".

He cautioned that, with the past emphasis on chasing paper qualifications, SkillsFuture Credit might face the pitfall of being used for the sake of acquiring qualifications, or to meet quotas/gain incentives instead of for equipping employees with the right skills that would really be utilised on the job. He cited an Organisation for Economic Cooperation and Development (OECD) survey of adult skills. Workers in Japan ranked highly in their skills but poorly as regards how well such skills are utilised on the job; conversely, US workers while ranking poorly in skills, were tops for utilising whatever skills they have to the fullest. Therefore, employers and employees must focus on the ends — acquiring, mastering and using deep skills that in turn can lead to higher productivity and wages.

Having an array of modular courses made available across educational and training institutions and at workplaces would mean individuals would be able to create their own learning pathways and unique skills maps. This could pose a challenge to Singaporeans, used to having roadmaps that were more fixed. It would become increasingly critical to move away from spoon-feeding the young to paving the way for them to become self-directed, resourceful and independent learners. Singaporeans need to seize learning opportunities everywhere, from anyone, throughout life and use their own initiative to do so.

The third major shift he saw was for Singaporeans to go beyond learning for work and to embrace learning for life. To quote Minister Heng's words, "Developing a lively interest in the world around us, in nature and culture, in sports and adventure, in having zest for life and a concern for others are what makes life purposeful and fulfilling".

Panellists at a post-Budget roundtable felt that the success of SkillsFuture lay primarily in the hands of individuals, stepping up to take responsibility for their own upgrading, with the support of companies.

An observation made during the roundtable was that educating Singaporeans about the importance of improving themselves would need to be a continuous affair, not a sporadic once a year or biannual effort. It would also take time to reap the benefits especially in the case of smaller firms that had no structured human resource strategy. The government might need to think of how to help these companies resolve their more immediate, pressing issues like the manpower crunch, which could hinder their participation in the SkillsFuture restructuring drive.

Professor Peter Cappelli, a management don from the University of Pennsylvania, also agreed that persuading employers would be difficult, albeit important. In a Straits Times article, he highlighted that employers in other countries had resisted training programmes as they perceived it to be too much work. He stressed that, over and above providing financial incentives, it would be critical to make access to these administratively easy so that employers will not be put off by any red tape, rules and regulations.

Few deny that there are still kinks to iron out for SkillsFuture and implementation issues to sort through. However, retaining the status quo in dealing with education and skills training may prove to be disastrous. In excerpts of his Budget Debate 2015, Minister Heng summed up the choices Singapore has before it succinctly as follows:

"We have two options. We could continue with the "study book" path, with a narrow focus on grades and examinations, and descend into a spiralling paper chase and expanding tuition industry. Employers choose not to invest in employees, relying wholly on academic qualifications to determine who gets the job. Educators drill and test, and see their duty as helping students to obtain the best possible examination grades. Parents obsess over grades and spend ever-increasing amounts of resources to give their child an edge over other children. Students chase the next point, and spend most of their time going for more tuition and enrichment in very narrow areas. Stress levels in society climb, and the system churns out students who excel in examinations, but are ill-equipped to take on jobs of the future, nor find fulfilment in what they do. And unemployment or under-employment becomes pervasive. Everyone is worse off.

This is a grim road, but sadly one in which other societies have already trodden down.

Or we can have another outcome. We can act with boldness and resolve to take another path forward, to embark on a major transformation. We will need collective will and action by employers, teachers, parents and students, and society at large, where employers look beyond academic qualifications in hiring and promoting the best person for the job; where bosses support employees in skills upgrading; where educators focus on holistic education, building a strong foundation of values and the capacity to learn; where our IHLs play a leading role strengthening the nexus between learning and work and learning for life; where parents recognise every child's unique strengths and do their part to build their children's character; where students flourish through a range of academic and co-curricular activities, and take different pathways to success and grow up to be well-rounded; where the economy stays resilient and flexible, with high levels of employment, and many opportunities — high skills, high productivity, high wages. And where our society and our people continue to be caring, harmonious, gracious and cohesive, and we do not see education as a race amongst our children.

This is a path that no society has charted out fully yet. Charting this new territory will require us to once again be pioneers."

SkillsFuture is an ambitious undertaking and challenges in implementing it would undoubtedly surface. However, it might also prove to be the secret weapon that Singapore needs to stay relevant and competitive in the constantly evolving global landscape.

If it succeeds even partially, then Singapore would once again have shown the way to the rest of the world, in creating a population that is continually learning, upgrading and reskilling, to keep up with the rapid changes in the economy, technology and society itself. The result of this would be a productive society, one that adds value from one generation to another, creating a virtuous cycle of economic growth and personal fulfilment.

CHAPTER 10

Key Lessons for Policy-Makers

In reviewing the history of the development of TVET in Singapore over the past fifty years, many aspects stand out. One is able to trace these in the narrative that has been presented in the foregoing chapters.

Training for the Job Market, Present and Future

When the PAP government took office in June 1959, it was faced with, among other issues, a high level of youth unemployment. Taken together with a high birthrate and a population demographic skewed towards those living on the margins with little education, this spelt potential social trouble if jobs could not be created quickly. The policy of rapid industrialization with high labour content was quickly determined as the solution, together with the training needed to fill these industrial-type jobs.

The British legacy of training clerks, typists and book-keepers to serve a mercantile economy was put to rest and instead courses in machining, wood-working, electrical wiring and mechanical drawing were quickly introduced. The government was not shy to request aid of a different kind, not in cash, but in the form of experts in training and instructional design for these early days. Local staff were mentored under these experts so that there was constant knowledge transfer.

The policy of closely linking technical and vocational training to market demand which started in 1959 has been the foundation for TVET policies ever since. Indeed, under EDB's guidance, training programmes were created to be ahead of demand in some cases. EDB intimately knew which industries were being targeted to be brought to Singapore in the early days of industrialization, and therefore training schemes were created to prepare trained manpower to meet these future needs. This proactive policy enabled many companies to become productive in a very short time and encouraged others to follow.

Today, all the ITE colleges as well as Polytechnic Schools have strong industry advisory committees to continue to provide feedback on the quality and characteristics of their graduates, the curriculum, equipment and facilities, internships, employment and so on. ITE has the DACUM[1] system of curriculum development, which requires it to send the curriculum to companies for their feedback and input and for industry representatives to sign off on the curriculum document.

It is also common for industry representatives to officiate at graduation ceremonies and speak to the new graduates to motivate them. Medals and prizes are sponsored by companies. Industry collaboration also extends to sponsorship or donation of equipment, scholarships and bursaries, industry-based projects, and the creation of real-life authentic learning environments. Industry also provide opportunities for instructors and lecturers to be attached to companies to understand their requirements better and also to bring the staff's knowledge up-to-date with the latest requirements as well as trends in the market.

The whole premise of TVET is directed towards market-based training. Although about 30% of the curriculum may be considered as soft-skills, even these are what are needed on the job and for career progress, such as teamwork, communication skills, problem-solving and ethical behavior.

A Strong Foundation at School

It took some time, until the early 1990's, to come to the realization that TVET students require at least 10 years of formal schooling with a solid grounding in language and mathematics. Prior to this, school dropouts and weak performers were being channeled to TVET. This did neither the student nor the system any good. Completion rates were low and the TVET system gained a poor reputation.

The change to 10 years of minimum schooling before TVET was a transformational policy. No longer was TVET seen as a poor alternative for academic failures. It began to be perceived as a legitimate post-secondary choice together with other routes, suitable for students with specific strengths and requirements. It took some years for the early damage to be undone, but unfortunately in many developing countries, TVET is still positioned at the bottom of the ladder. This is highly demotivating for students as well as damaging for the employers who have to employ them.

---

[1] Developing a Curriculum (DACUM) is a process that incorporates the use of a focus group to take into account the major duties and tasks required in an occupation, along with the necessary knowledge, skills, and traits. This cost-effective method results in an effective and thorough analysis of any job.

Clarity of Purpose

Post-secondary education in Singapore is characterised by clarity and flexibility. Students who apply to the Institute of Technical Education, Polytechnics, Junior Colleges and Universities know precisely the kind of education, level of skills and outcomes that they can expect, even the kind of jobs and careers that they are likely to find themselves in. However, they also know that there is a system of bridges and ladders which allows them to move to the next level of education if they meet the requisite eligibility criteria in a competitive environment.

Meanwhile, the institutions are sufficiently autonomous to make changes to their program offerings and intakes to reflect changing realities and needs. These include hybrid programmes, internships, overseas attachments, problem-based learning, and entrepreneurship development. Examples of such hybrid programmes are those combining ICT with business, design with manufacturing systems, electronic and mechanical systems, law and economics and so on.

These rapid adjustments in school education policies and curriculum as well as at post-secondary and tertiary level, have resulted in graduate employment rates of close to 90%, even as the economy continued to restructure every decade.

Excellent Campus Facilities

Visitors to the three ITE colleges and the five polytechnics in Singapore marvel at the scale, design and facilities provided, which are not usually associated with TVET institutes but more with universities in developed countries.

In many cases, these campuses are master-planned by internationally-renowned architects. For example, the Temasek Polytechnic campus was planned by James Stirling Michael Wilford partners of London, the Nanyang Polytechnic campus by Gwathmey Siegel Kaufman Architects of the US and the Republic Polytechnic campus by Fumihiko Maki of Japan. The ITE campuses were also designed by top local architects with a global presence; ITE Colleges East, Central, and HQ by RSP Architects and Engineers, and ITE College West by DPA Architects.

Typically each of these campuses would, in addition to the standard teaching facilities of lecture theatres, laboratories, workshops, staff offices and restaurants, also feature outstanding sports facilities, studios and theatres for the arts and cultural activities, auditoria of various capacities, media studios, shops, restaurants, travel agencies, and many other specialized facilities. The sports facilities include Olympic-sized swimming pools, indoor sports halls, athletic stadia which are used for football, rugby and hockey, rock-climbing walls, and so on. Temasek Polytechnic boasts an artificial turf hockey pitch as well as a nearby body of water for kayaking and round-the-lake cross-country races.

Most are located close to transport nodes like mass rapid transit stations and are accessible by public transport.

The Temasek Polytechnic campus next to Bedok reservoir could easily clinch the title of the most beautiful polytechnic campus in the world. Designed around a central horseshoe-shaped plaza, and with gardens, koi-filled ponds, a fountain and colourful corridors, it is the anti-thesis of the standard image of a polytechnic in anyone's mind.

Many centres of excellence have been established in these campuses, in areas such as IT security, biotechnology, culinary skills, robotics and so on, all with leading industry partners. For students who are studying at these campuses, the activities available after classes are enormous and varied, from community service to choirs, from dance to dragon boat racing. Therefore discipline problems are fewer. Students are occupied by a myriad of activities on campus.

With such facilities, it is not surprising that ITE and Polytechnic students can be found sporting Singapore colours at various regional and international games such as soccer, athletics, swimming, WorldSkills, and other events. This in turn raises the profile of these institutions further, attracting like-minded students.

Genuine and Generous Government Support

Since independence, the Singapore government has been steadily increasing its support of TVET through expansion and investments. While many other governments recognize the importance of this sector of education for economic and social growth and development, in terms of actual commitment and investment, only lip-service has been paid. Not only has investment been poor, there is a paucity of good instructors, no career path for staff, and a heavy dependence on part-timers or adjuncts. Principals and lecturers have not been upgraded and have little experience in industry.

At ITE and Polytechnics in Singapore, as government statutory boards, the pay scales follow closely that of the government civil service. There are proper appraisal systems, career development plans, upgrading of skills and knowledge and regular reviews to ensure that the total package is competitive. After all, all lecturers and instructors are recruited from business and industry, so their compensation and benefits have to be competitive with the overall market.

In terms of budget, the government pays for all capital expenditures such as buildings, facilities and equipment. It also covers about 80–85% of the operating costs of running each institution. The fees collected from students only covers the remaining 15–20% of the operating and manpower costs. Notwithstanding this, there are regular fee increases to keep up with wage costs and higher operating costs.

Each campus (based on the last three polytechnics to be built and the three ITE campuses) is estimated to have cost about USD200–300M to build and equip. In addition, each has been designed to be a showcase or icon in architectural design and technology. In terms of size, each ITE campus can accommodate about 8,000–10,000 students, while each Polytechnic is built for a capacity 13,500 students. Therefore, there are great economies of scale built into each of the campuses, while being able to provide facilities like auditoria, sports complexes and student centres which would otherwise not be tenable in a smaller campus.

Support from government is not just in the form of budget allocations. The government also appoints very eminent, highly respected and experienced people on the boards of each of the institutions to ensure that they are managed with the highest level of probity and integrity, and meet the needs of business and industry. The boards are always tripartite in nature, representing employers, unions and various arms of the government. That such senior business people are involved in the trusteeship of the TVET institutions is a strong signal to the public of the standards to be expected.

Gender Equality and Image

One of the key features of technical education in Singapore is that it attracts equal proportions of men and women to study in the various institutions. This is because of the wide range of programmes on offer, not limited to only hard technical disciplines like engineering and technology. Courses in business, applied sciences, allied health, media, communications, ICT, tourism and hospitality, food technology and legal studies attract both genders. Even in engineering, the number of female students is about 40% as a significant number of job functions such as engineering design, planning and control, and building management do not require outdoor work.

This provides for a more vibrant campus environment with a large and diverse range of activities as well as a balanced workforce in business and industry. Most importantly, it totally redefines the term technical education, away from the traditional image to one which is much more inclusive, broader, more diverse and more exciting to young people.

Open Bridges and Ladders for Upgrading

A critical factor in the success story of TVET in Singapore is the structure of bridges and ladders that permeate the whole system. Regardless of where one may start from in the educational hierarchy, there will always be pathways available towards higher levels of attainment of skills and knowledge. This can be through part-time or full-time study. Polytechnic diploma holders may study towards advanced or specialist diplomas or degrees. ITE certificate holders may enroll in a polytechnic diploma course, and over time, to a degree.

No qualification need be seen as a terminal point. Many TVET graduates have achieved doctoral degrees overseas and returned as lecturers.

This system of bridges and ladders provides a strong motivation and drive to students to do well in their studies and to take their training seriously. Scholarships and bursaries are available to good students to keep upgrading themselves.

Authentic and Innovative Learning Environments

Students who are less academic but more kinesthetic or visual usually need different approaches to learning. The TVET institutions are particularly good at this. Throughout the campuses, one can find student-run cafes and restaurants, kitchens, retail outlets, banks, travel agencies and even clean rooms for semiconductor fabrication. These provide students with opportunities to express their creativity and imagination, practise interdisciplinary group work and build their confidence in fitting into a work environment easily.

There are also different pedagogical innovations of diverse kinds. Problem-based learning or PBL is used at Temasek Polytechnic and Republic Polytechnic. Nanyang Polytechnic specializes in industry-based projects for students, Singapore Polytechnic is well-established for design-thinking, while Ngee Ann Polytechnic has developed a strong focus on Arts Management. Such a variety of approaches is possible as each institution is autonomous for its own curriculum and assessment and award of its diplomas. There is no requirement for standardized testing or results. However, each jealously guards its standards and acceptance by industry. Job placement figures and starting salaries are published annually, so public comparisons can be made easily. This ensures that the awards of each institution are maintained at a high standard and are not allowed to depreciate.

About 50% of each cohort also get an overseas training opportunity at least once during their course of study. This provides them with an experience that many would not otherwise have had on their own. These could be in the form of attachments or internships with companies overseas.

Strong Business Links

Each TVET institution maintains close ties with business and industry. From the composition of the managing board to the various advisory committees, business and industry representatives are appointed to provide the senior management with guidance and contacts. These board members serve on the HR or Administrative Committees which decides on staff recruitment, pay and promotion policies. Hence, industry representatives even have a say on the qualifications and experience of those who are recruited as lecturers. As members of the Audit and Finance committees, they also approve financial policies and ensure compliance with financial regulations.

But more than that, as mentioned, business and industry also provide attachment places for students and lecturers, help in setting occupational standards and establishing centres of excellence in training, and give advice in a broad range of ways.

This nexus between the training institutions and employers therefore ensures that the institution is able to foresee and respond to changing trends in the real world. At the end of the day, it ensures that the graduates are what employers are looking for, both for their immediate requirements as well as to meet their projected needs in the future.

Competition among Institutions

With five polytechnics offering about 50 different diploma programmes each, and each operating autonomously, there is intense competition for students and staff. This creates an environment of constant innovation and improvement in the provision of services to students and industry collaboration. Although all come under the same umbrella of the Ministry of Education and all are considered equal in funding, there is an unwritten pegging order which translates to quality of students and graduates.

This internal competitive spirit removes any remnant of complacency or sense of staying put with the status quo. There is a constant churning of new ideas and experiments in pedagogy. When an idea works well, these are adopted quickly by the other institutions so the "first-mover" advantage does not last longer than a year in this market.

This competition is not just to see who can use the best methods and technologies to produce the best learning outcomes, but also in the areas of character development, community service, service learning, global and cultural sensitivity, and readiness for a future which is constantly changing. Whether in education, arts or sports, each institution develops its own creative way to engage its students, keep them motivated and imbue them with a spirit of civic duty.

Thus by providing autonomy to issue their own diplomas according to their own curriculum and standards, the government has shown faith in the integrity of each institution and allowed them to flourish without a heavy hand, such as a standardized programme or curriculum.

TVET as a Post-Secondary Route

One of the eye-opening lessons that Singapore has learnt is that TVET requires its own identity and branding as a post-secondary option, much like the Swiss–German model. It should not become a catch-all option for dropouts from school. This lesson was learnt the hard way, after many cohorts of students had been affected by the earlier policy that vocational education and training would be good for those who were academically-weak and hence dropping out of school.

This was a lose-lose solution, as students thought of VET as a last resort option and were not motivated; the institutions found that the students were under-prepared in language skills and mathematics; and finally, employers were not satisfied with the quality of the graduates. Meanwhile, the dropout rates from the vocational institutes clearly indicated a wastage of scarce human resources. This was corrected in the early 1990's through the introduction of mandatory 10-years of schooling for everyone and the establishment of the Institute of Technical Education (ITE) as a post-secondary institution. With that, 90% of every cohort was able to progress to post-secondary education, with 65% going to polytechnics or ITE and 25% to Junior Colleges which is the direct route to University.

Integrated Manpower Planning

The Council for Professional and Technical Education (CPTE), chaired by the Minister for Trade and Industry and comprising other Ministers, would approve the macro-planning of places in post-secondary education. The number of places in ITE, Polytechnics and the professional schools of the Universities would be set in broad terms. The individual institutions then could spread these broad targets among different programmes according to their own strengths. Thus, there was a straight line of sight between long-term economic goals, investment flows and manpower supply ahead of time. This was important given the time lag in training.

Lately, retraining for employed or displaced persons in new skills has taken on a greater urgency as the labour markets have shown increased volatility, in parallel with the global economy. Hence policies to update skills and training have been introduced to incentivise those affected to go for retraining. The new mantra of continuous education and training is gaining ground quickly as companies and individuals need to be fleet-footed to survive in Singapore's globalised economy.

The economic development strategy and the manpower planning that goes with it is a two-way street, with VET managers involved in understanding the strategies. Thus the process is not top-down instruction, but one which involves feedback from the institutions as well.

Competent and Professional Implementation

While it is easy to formulate policy and pass regulations, there has to be competent and professional people who can implement these policies on the ground successfully. The choice of competent academic leaders who can execute policy with panache and clarity is a key aspect of Singapore's educational landscape. At every institution, there are committed and passionate people who are able to lead, plan and implement the overall policy intentions with great skill and drive. That this has happened over many decades shows that at every level, correct appraisal of an individual's capability as well as good succession planning, are key. Regardless of race, language or religion, talent is allowed to flow upwards and is not sidelined. This is truly one of Singapore's greatest strengths and assets.

Conclusion

Singapore's TVET journey has been exciting and varied. It has been characterized by prudent experimentation, bold decision-making, focused commitment to job-creation and people development. However, the journey is not over. As the world economy moves to a new and unpredictable phase of volatility and dynamic change, Singapore also has to be nimble enough to change course. A single skill is insufficient to ensure life-long employability. Rather, a set of generic skill-sets and the capability to learn and adapt to changing circumstances will be key. This is an entirely new paradigm and Singapore has just begun its next stage of development in this area.

One can however be optimistic that Singapore starts this new phase from a position of strength and when the next update of TVET development is written, it will record another unique transformational story, except that it will happen in 25, not 50 years.

Bibliography

Chan Chieu Kiat, et al, (1961), Report of the Commission of Enquiry into Vocational and Technical Education in Singapore, State of Singapore.

Cheeseman, H.R. (1938), Report on Vocational Education in Malaya.

Chiang, Mickey (1998), "From Economic Debacle to Economic Miracle", 1998, Ministry of Education, Singapore.

Dobby, E.H.G et al. (1953), Report of the Committee on a Polytechnic Institute for Singapore, State of Singapore.

Gan Kim Yong, et al (2006), Report of the Polytechnic-School Review Committee: Expanding Applied Learning Options, Government of Singapore.

Goh Keng Swee et al. (1979), Report on the Ministry of Education, Government of Singapore.

Gopinathan, S. (1999), Preparing, for the Next Rung; Economic Restructuring and Education Reform in Singapore. *J Education and Work*. **12**(3). 295–308.

Institute of Technical Education (1994), Improving Worker Training: Report of the CET Review Team.

Institute of Technical Education, (2012), Reliving ITE's Transformation, ITE Singapore.

Kynnerseley, C.W.S. et al. (1902), Report of the Commission of Enquiry into the system of English Education in the Colony.

Law Song Seng (2008), Vocational Technical Education and Economic Development: The Singapore Experience. In Lee S.K., Goh C.B., B. Fredriksen, Tan J.P. (eds), *Towards a Better Future: Education and Training for Economic development in Singapore Since 1965* (pp 114–134). Washington DC, The World Bank.

Law Song Seng (2015), A Breakthrough in Vocational and Technical Education, The Singapore Story, World Scientific and Institute of Policy Studies, Singapore.

Lemon, A.H. et al (1919), Report of the Committee on Technical and Industrial Education in the Federated Malay States.

Lim Kok Hua (1988), The Ngee Ann Story: The First 25 Years, Ngee Ann Polytechnic.

Lim Swee Say (2011), Surviving the Great Recession, in *Heart Work* 2, Economic Development Board, Singapore.

Shelley, R.A. et al, Report of the Review Committee on Technical Education in Secondary Schools, Ministry of Education.

Singapore Polytechnic (2005), Opening Minds, Shaping Lives, The Journey of Singapore's First Polytechnic, Singapore Polytechnic.

Tan, Sumiko (2004), First and Foremost: Training Technologists for the Nation: Forty years of the Singapore Polytechnic.

Technical Education Department (1971), Education and Training of Engineers, Technicians and Craftsmen and Operatives in Singapore, Ministry of Education, Singapore.

Toh Peng Kiat (1968), The Scope of Vocational and Technical Education in Singapore, Economic Research Paper 1/68, Ministry of Finance, Singapore.

Tucker, Mark. (2012), The Phoenix: Vocational Education and Training in Singapore. Washington DC: National Centre on Education and the Economy.

Vocational and Industrial Training Board (1991), Upgrading Vocational Training, VITB, Singapore.

Winstedt, R.O. (1917), Report on the Vernacular and Industrial Education in the Netherlands, East Indies and the Phillipines.

Winstedt, R.O. et al, (1925), Report of the Technical Education Committee.

Yip, John, et al. (1991), Report of the Review Committee on Improving Primary Education.

Index